'In this, Andy's third book, l[...]
versal longing for a sense o[...]
himself lives in a state of com[...]
Spirit – and we are made in [...] surprise that
we, too, are designed for community in a literal and spiritual
sense. What might that look like? Is it static? Are there other
facets to belonging? Andy believes this is "a journey", and truly,
to discover our God-given identity and purpose is the crucial
starting point for everything else on our life-long pilgrimage.

'Drawing on his own upbringing, family life and biblical
examples, Andy colours an attractive picture of God's desires
for us, recognising that the constraints of language can't always
adequately express the vastness of the majesty and immeasura-
ble love of God: "Like pouring a pint of water into a half-pint
glass, there will always be more than we could possibly ever
hold." Exactly. Nevertheless, he gently points the way for us to
enjoy multiple aspects of belonging, prompting us to remember that "belonging is rooted in the very heart of God himself,
who is calling us, wooing us, reaching for us in every single
moment." It's a timely reminder.'

Jenny Sanders, international speaker,
prophetic teacher and author

'The human need to belong has perhaps never felt so pressing
as it does today, yet we also see with painful clarity how harmful blind tribalism can be. Now, as a global pandemic forces
us to isolate from each other, we are, ironically, finding creative ways towards a deeper re-connection with each other, with
creation and with the mystery we call God. Using a wealth of
personal experience and scriptural illustration, Andy expertly
guides and compassionately accompanies us along authentic
pathways of belonging.'

Margaret Silf, author and retreat facilitator

'*Made to Belong* casts a vision for belonging in unity that answers the cry deep in each of our hearts to know and be known and is very much needed in today's fractured society, especially after the trials of lockdown and isolation. If you've ever felt you don't belong or fit in, and that's probably most of us, you need to read this book! I appreciated the wonderful journey Andy takes us on to discover what it means to belong, using biblical characters and sharing his own life story. It will not only provoke you to think deeply about where and how we each belong but also to think more about how you can help others to belong too. You will be inspired and encouraged by this book as you continue your journey to find your true connection to God, to each other and to the world.'

Penelope Swithinbank, Anglican clergy and author

'Andy tackles one of the deepest and most meaningful instincts in the hearts of men and women. Almost all of us want to belong – to something. Andy takes his readers on a carefully planned journey of discovery towards the place where ultimate safety and true community are created and prepared for us. A warm, well-crafted and very timely gift to the Church.'

Adrian Plass, speaker and author

'*Made to Belong* is a tonic to the soul. A route map to reconnection with ourselves, with each other and with God. Andy Percey's down-to-earth and masterful combination of scholarship and common sense exposes the many masks that the ugly face of tribalism disguises itself in as he explores the beauty and power of the Bible's revolutionary assertion that "we" are created in God's image, the image that defines humanity as a whole.'

Steve Chalke, Founder and Leader of Oasis Global

'In a world filled with people who ache for togetherness, and where carnage is quietly wrought by loneliness, Andy gently but powerfully points us to the way it was always meant to be: belonging. Laced with grace, his words are insightful and practical. Highly recommended.'

Jeff Lucas, author, speaker and broadcaster

'Needing to belong is fundamental to our mental and emotional wellbeing. The Covid-19 pandemic, with the isolation that has resulted, has served to highlight this even more strongly, which makes Andy's book very timely.'

Jeannie Kendall, writer and speaker

'Anything that Andy Percey writes is worth reading. And in this more conversational book he raises one of the most controversial issues of our day: the need to belong without the need to exclude. *Made to Belong* is an important Christian response to the debate.'

Ian Stackhouse, Senior Pastor of Millmead and author

'With loneliness and isolation at epidemic levels, this book helps us to grapple with God's best for us – we are indeed "made to belong". I believe these pages will recalibrate your heart, and give opportunity for self-reflection, theological understanding and practical action. Andy powerfully reminds us all that we are part of God's divine relationship restoration plan. Highly recommended.'

Cathy Madavan, speaker, broadcaster and author

'In an age when radical individualism undermines community and social media distracts from self-giving friendship, this book reminds us that a sense of belonging is basic to a sense of identity.'

John E Cowell, author

Made to Belong

Moving beyond tribalism to find our true connection in God

Andy Percey

Authentic

First published 2021 by Authentic Media Limited,
PO Box 6326, Bletchley, Milton Keynes, MK1 9GG.
authenticmedia.co.uk

The right of Andy Percey to be identified as the Author of this Work
has been asserted by him in accordance with the
Copyright, Designs and Patents Act 1988.

British Library Cataloguing in Publication Data
A catalogue record for this book is available from the British Library.
ISBN: 978-1-78893-185-4
978-1-78893-186-1 (e-book)

Unless otherwise stated, Scripture quotes are taken from the New Revised Standard
Version Bible: Anglicised Edition, copyright © 1989, 1995 the Division of Christian
Education of the National Council of the Churches of Christ in the United States of
America. Used by permission. All rights reserved.

Scripture quotations from *The Message*, copyright © 1993, 2002, 2018 by Eugene
H. Peterson. Used by permission of NavPress. All rights reserved. Represented by
Tyndale House Publishers, Inc.

Scripture quotations marked 'NIV' are taken from the Holy Bible, New
International Version (Anglicised edition), copyright © 1979, 1984, 2011 by Biblica.
Used by permission of Hodder & Stoughton Publishers, an Hachette UK company.
All rights reserved.
'NIV' is a registered trademark of Biblica UK trademark number 1448790.

Scripture quotations from The Authorized (King James) Version. Rights in the
Authorized Version in the United Kingdom are vested in the Crown. Reproduced by
permission of the Crown's patentee, Cambridge University Press.

Scripture quotations marked 'NLV' are taken from the New Life Version, copyright
© 1969 and 2003. Used by permission of Barbour Publishing, Inc., Uhrichsville,
Ohio 44683. All rights reserved.

Cover design by Vivian Hansen
Printed and bound by CPI Group (UK) Ltd, Croydon, CR0 4YY

Acknowledgements

As always, there are lots of people to thank because, without their support and encouragement, this book would never have been printed.

Donna and the wonderful team at Authentic. You are a wonderful and supportive team, and you do amazing work – thank you for all your encouraging help.

Charlie, John, Jeannie, Ian and Tim for their honesty, wisdom and for sharing with me in this journey.

As always, my incredible wife Bex. Your gentle wisdom has made this a better book, and your love and support has once again given me the courage to write. Thank you for all the ways you have taught me what it means to belong and for nurturing that space of belonging in our lives. I love you with all my heart.

To my darling son Leo. Thank you that you continue to teach me what matters and to find joy in the simple yet profound things in life. You teach me every day how to be a better man and father, and I am so proud to be your daddy.

Andy Percey
Summer, 2020

For our beautiful son Leo.

May you always know a place to belong, and may it give you
the strength to go out into the world courageously and shine.

Contents

Foreword

It was about a year ago when I first met Andy. We had the same publisher, and after learning that there were 'two of us' living in the city of Bath, we decided to meet and talk about ministry and the highs (along with a few lows) of writing books.[1]

One of the first things I noticed about him was a sense that he was comfortable in his own skin – this was not someone trying to impress, nor was he trying to hide. We had a good chat about living in Bath, life in ministry, his wife and young son, and writing books.

After finishing our coffee, I was hastily grabbing my handbag – already thinking about my next meeting – while he calmly remained seated, explaining that his afternoon was free because he was working that evening. My glazed look of utter confusion was his first clue that I had no comprehension of an evening meeting justifying an afternoon off.

Having noticed my brain was in a bit of a twist (perhaps the furrowed brow gave it away), Andy began explaining that he likes to break the day into thirds – working two thirds but leaving the other third for resting and for his family. He even mentioned practising a five-day working week . . . as a pastor! I honestly thought he was either a bit lazy or a bit mad.

It certainly sounded like a quaint idea and my exhausted self was eager to voice approval for such a practice, but I quickly rebuked any thought of a new rhythm; I had far too much work to do . . . let's not complicate matters by actually resting.

Yet, after reading his second book, *Infused with Life*, I realized the error in my ways and the wisdom in his. Here was someone who had learned from his mistakes, was honest about his struggles and who had a heart to help others walk into the freedom he has discovered.

Therefore, when Andy asked me to write the foreword for his next book, I was eager to see what topic he had chosen to tackle. I knew that my own sense of comfort might be unsettled but the cost would likely be worth the unease, and I was proved right.

The matter of belonging is not a new topic, but I believe it is a timely one.

From the beginning of time, humanity has fought against exclusion, seeking acceptance and validation, regardless of the cost. Whether it was Adam and Eve in the Garden of Eden, the disciples vying to sit at the right hand of Jesus or our own attempts to ensure inclusion to a culture, church, relationship or 'inner circle', we have all wondered at one time or another: am I necessary?

In the years prior to 2020, social media had begun to overshadow the need for belonging with the desire for approval; in other words, approval equalled belonging. This shallow basis for acceptance made the world more competitive – comparing our holidays, children, lifestyles and even restaurant food – to the point where authenticity often bowed to marketability. Reality was not as important as response, with daily life regularly edited and filtered so only the highlight reel made the cut. The increase in 'likes' justified the lack of integrity in posts. This was not the case for everyone by any means, but it was the temptation of many – a temptation which increased our desire for inclusivity at the expense of our own sincerity.

Facing the pandemic of 2020 and seeing the world turned upside down, as it were, cemented the question of necessity even further in our psyche. With an entire population put into lockdown, those workers who may have previously been overlooked suddenly acquired increased importance, and those who formerly felt secure in their statuses were now confronted with potential redundancy. Not only that, the term 'necessary' became dictated by those in authority rather than the lure of popularity.

This cultural shift has begun dusting off the distraction of approval, leaving us to face, once again, the question of what it means to really belong.

In short, at least in the western world, we may be returning from 'am I enough?' (a need for approval) back to 'am I necessary?' (a need for existence). Andy presents the answer to both painfully honest questions when he writes, 'You have been created in love, to be loved.'

It is a simple yet equally challenging statement which generates a variety of questions: what does this type of love look like? Can we fully receive God's love while still battling our doubts, sins, and weaknesses? How do we love others this way without demanding change? What does it look like to love creation as well as the Creator? What would the Bride of Christ look like if she truly knew – and believed – the Creator's love for her? Through his understated yet profound writing, we learn how Andy navigated his own journey of discovery, seeking answers to these questions and more.

Made to Belong is spiritually enriching, theologically challenging and personally uplifting. It may stir the waters of your past but will simultaneously point you towards the hope of your future.

More than anything, I believe this book will capture the truth of God's heart for his children, answering the deep cry of our humanity, leading us towards this simple truth: we belong.

Jen Baker
Author/Speaker
Bath, England

1

Sitting Around the Fire

*'From cave paintings to video games, we are
story-making and storytelling creatures.'*[1]

Since our earliest days, human beings have sat around the tribal
fires and told stories. Stories about where we came from and
where we are going; stories about how we belong. We want
to not only have the answers to those big questions of life but
to share those answers with others, and in that sharing, weave
ourselves into a richer and more vibrant tapestry. This desire is
deeply built into us, more deeply than we are often aware of or
can understand. The glow of that tribal fire is enticing.

We recently had a flyer come through our door entitled
'Finding Your Tribe'. To be honest, it made a welcome change
from the rainforest's worth of local-election leaflets that had
landed there in the weeks before and after. It was an invitation to women aged 45–65 to make connections with friends
in Bath.

Now there are dozens of groups like this around the city, and
many of them will use similar words like *connection* or a *circle
of friendship*, but what was it about this language of 'Tribe' that
means this flyer is still on my desk weeks later, even though I
am a man in my thirties?

The answer, as best as I can understand it, is that there is something very powerful about tribes. We all want to belong, to have a connection, to feel part of something; we want to have satisfied that deep longing in the fabric of our being to be rooted.

Rise of Tribalism in Our World Today

As a football fan, I have often been surrounded by an element of tribalism. Thankfully I was born after some of the terrible violence that was seen around football grounds when tribalism was fierce. Thankfully now it is mostly good natured. I have supported Tottenham Hotspur for over thirty years and was overjoyed when, in the 2018/19 season, we reached the Champions League final (the premier competition in European club football). We played Liverpool, and at the time, Bex, Leo and I were on holiday with my parents in Pembrokeshire, South Wales. My dad and I did our homework and found a pub in St Davids where we could watch the game. To say that there was a gathering of Tottenham fans would be a gross overstatement; I think I saw two or three others. The other one hundred people in the pub were all wearing Liverpool shirts as if the entire South Wales Liverpool Supporters Club had decided, along with us four Tottenham fans, that this was the pub for them. My dad is a Southampton fan and I think he was laughing.

Despite the tribal loyalties at the highest level of competition and despite the alcohol flowing in the pub, the conversation and the banter remained good natured. Sadly, the performance of my team was not, and we lost the game 2–0.

In my childhood, tribalism seemed to be confined to sport. It didn't seem as though tribalism played a very important role in society; I was too young to really know what was going on in the world or in politics.

And, perhaps, there is the challenge. These issues of tribalism, that are as old as human beings themselves, have always been there. I have just been unaware of them and their importance – of the allure of that fire.

There seems to have been a resurgence of tribalism in our world today.

That enticing glow has become somewhat of a raging fire. As I look around today, I see tribalism everywhere. Between social groups and even within social groups, politics, and faith.

We have seen a rise in nationalism around the world. The shrinking of a common global project and the narrowing down to national agenda. There would be some who would say that this is what the debate around Brexit has been about.

Whichever way you voted in that referendum in 2016, *Leave* or *Remain*, there was a tribal element to those endless debates which centred around the big questions of who we are, where we have come from and where are we going. Whether those questions were hijacked by those agendas on either side is another matter and are questions which many are tired of.

In some ways, there is both a strength and a problem with a referendum, and they stem from the same point. The question is usually binary.[2] In the case of the 2016 referendum on the United Kingdom's membership of the European Union, it was 'should we leave or remain?'. This was the strength of the question. It seems straightforward. Two choices. Until you see the challenge. This is not a binary issue, and the questions, emotions, politics, history, economics surrounding this one binary question are anything but binary.

The challenge we will see in the coming chapters as we explore what it means to be made to belong, is that these issues are rarely binary.

I am sorry to mention Brexit so early on in the book, and I can assure you that it isn't going to feature much, if at all, in the pages that follow. It does, however, highlight the tribal nature of those debates and our culture more widely at the moment, and more troublingly, reveals an 'us against them' mentality which seems to be at the very heart of so many societies around the world today. Tribalism has, at its heart, a binary expression.

Why is Tribalism Important?

Lions have prides, wolves have packs and baboons have troops. I could go on. I am sure that many of you familiar with quizzes will have, at some point, had a round come up asking you what you call a certain group of animals. Did you know that a group of ravens is called an unkindness and a group of crows is called a murder? That's the last time I put birdseed out in the garden!

It is not good for the human to be alone

Human beings have tribes. However, there are similarities between human social behaviour and animal social behaviour, and this should not surprise us as we are part of the same created system. For a wolf, being part of the pack gives it the protection of the others and the power of the collective in a hunt. The same goes for the lion and the pride. There are benefits from being in the group, and there are negatives when outside it. The same is true of human beings, and tribes have given us that social and physical protection for thousands of years.

When we go back to the Genesis poem in the Bible, the first human being is taken from the dust of the earth and placed at the centre of the garden. This human being was linked though biology and chemistry to the world that it was a part of. However, something was missing. We see the account in Genesis 2:

> And the LORD God fashioned from the soil each beast of the field and each fowl of the heavens and brought each to the human to see what he would call it, and whatever the human called a living creature, that was its name. And the human called names to all the cattle and to the fowl of the heavens and to all the beasts of the field, but for the human no sustainer beside him was found.[3]

Standing on the balcony in Verona, Juliet asks the question, 'What's in a name?' There is something significant and relational about naming. If you have children, then you will know that choosing a name is not always straightforward and can be a lengthy process, precisely because it is significant. Here in the garden, the human being is given the role of naming the animals in order to find a partner, or 'helper' as we often find it translated. But there is still something missing.

> And the LORD God cast a deep slumber on the human, and he slept, and He took one of his ribs and closed over the flesh where it had been, and the Lord God built the rib He had taken from the human into a woman and He brought her to the human. And the human said: 'This one at last, bone of my bones and flesh of my flesh, this one shall be called Woman, for from man was this one taken.' Therefore does a man leave his father and his mother and cling to his wife and they shall become one flesh.[4]

I want to say from the start, as we are thinking about how human beings relate to each other, what we might take from the word 'helper'. As I look at the text in Genesis 2 and I look throughout the Bible, then I come to the conclusion that this is both a significant and important role, not a subservient one. Partnership between human beings, expressed here as that between a man and a woman, is not one that puts one above the other. For those who might be tempted to see 'helper' as a subservient role, then we need look no further than the Psalms:

We wait in hope for the LORD; he is our *help* and our shield.[5]

Both the words used in Genesis and here in the Psalms come from the same root word.

In fact, according to Hebrew scholar Robert Alter, the word '"help" is too weak because it suggests a merely auxiliary function . . .'[6] Alter prefers to translate the word as 'sustainer'. That here, alongside, opposite and as a counterpart to this first human, is another of the same who can be a sustainer.

Partnership, from the very beginning, has been about something deeper than chemistry and biology. The first human being has chemistry and biology that is in harmony with the rest of creation, but something was still missing. Relationship. Partnership. Companionship. Belonging. The words that bubble out of the first human on finding this partner is almost like a song. There is a recognition that something has been found, that forever they are not just two among many in the garden but that these two are now one.

What we see here at the beginning is that God has placed, deep within humanity, a desire to belong. A desire not just to be recognized in the other but to be found there also.

My wife Bex is half Kiwi. Her mum, Glenys, moved to the UK at the age of 21 after she got married, but almost all of her family remain in New Zealand. It is a beautiful country that we have been blessed to visit since we have been married, and we will one day go back with Leo to show him where some of his roots are. Bex's uncle is Wayne, who is a Maori. Many of you may not know much about the Maori other than the famous war dance, or Hakka, which the All Blacks (the nickname for the New Zealand Rugby Union team) perform before every match. In truth, I didn't know all that much either.

Recently, Bex's aunty Meryl and uncle Wayne came to visit us in Bath, and during a meal at a local restaurant, I was able to ask Wayne more about his Maori culture and what it means to belong to it. What I learned was that Maori society is strongly rooted in a sense of collective (tribal) belonging, underpinned by each member's knowledge of their links and attachments to kinship groups. This is anchored by a relationship to common ancestral lines, historical events, geographical points and an all-encompassing spiritual dimension.

Let me give you an example that Wayne gave me to illustrate the point. When a Maori is giving a speech at a Marae,[7] they will usually acknowledge the Supreme Being, the Earth Mother, those who have departed, the place where they are standing and the Meeting House.

This would then be followed by expressing their ties or relationships to particular major geographical points such as mountains and rivers. This would then be followed by identifying their ancestral lines and tribal areas. The point of beginning in this way is that it establishes the identity of the speaker, where they are from and where they belong.

I learned during the meal that it is rude within Maori culture to ask a person what they 'do'. What is important within the culture is 'who you are', which is defined in all the ways I have just mentioned. A person within Maori culture does not live in isolation or simply out of a place of past connection.

They live within a society, a group that is united on the basis of family ties, sharing life together where each member has a role, performs a function and serves the improvement of the group and those in it. It is in that loyalty, caring, sharing and the fulfilling of your responsibilities to the group that you find yourself. Jack Donovan speaks of this in his book *Becoming a Barbarian*:

> To become part of a tribe, you must be willing to let go of one version of yourself . . . and find another version of yourself within the group.[8]

Or in the famous words of St Francis of Assisi:

> For it is in giving that we receive; it is in pardoning that we are pardoned; it is in dying that we are born again to eternal life.

It is in this idea of finding yourself within the tribe, through those who are part of it with you, that some of the best of tribalism can be found.

At the very core of who we are as human beings, at the source and since the very beginning, we have within us the desire not only to connect but to belong. According to developmental psychologist Susan Pinker:

> The universal hunger to connect and belong explains much of human behaviour from birth until death. Our very survival depends on it.[9]

Because this is often a matter of life and death, of survival, it is easy to get enticed into drawing battle lines. All of a sudden, we start to see beyond the differences we have and start to see people themselves as different. All of a sudden, it is not 'we' who are working through the issues we face, it is 'us' and 'them'. As writer David Berreby puts it in his article in *National Geographic*:

> It's a common misfortune around the world: People get along well enough for decades, even centuries, across lines of race or religion or culture. Then, suddenly, the neighbours aren't people you respect, invite to dinner, trade favours with, or marry. Those once familiar faces are now Them, the Enemy, the Other. And in that clash of groups, individuality vanishes and empathy dries up, as does trust. It can happen between herders and farmers in Nigeria or between native-born people and immigrants in France or the United States.[10]

We not only see this all around the world but we see it in our communities, our work places and even our families.

A Fence or a Well?

When I was twenty, I travelled around Australia and Thailand with a friend. It was a fantastic experience which opened my eyes to different cultures and people – I loved it.

When we first arrived in Australia, we landed in Perth, on the western coast. During our stay in Western Australia, we spent some time on a massive ranch where they kept a large herd of cattle. It was an amazing experience to muster the cattle on a quad bike and to ride out to the boundaries of the land to check that everything was ok.

There is a challenge with this type of farming, though. How do you build a fence around such a large amount of land? It is very difficult, and expensive; many choose not to and to adopt a different model. I'll come on to that in a moment. Here in the UK, where plots of land are generally smaller, we tend to build fences or walls. The boundaries serve the purpose of keeping your animals in – and any animals you don't want to come in, out. It is about protection and preservation, and the wall achieves that goal.

However, when the land is very large and you cannot build a fence or a wall, what is the solution? Many farmers in these situations will build a well, or a watering hole, and place it at the centre of the land because they know that the animals will never stray far away from where the water is. The water is life. The animals will never stray far away from where the life is!

Think about this in the context of tribalism. Tribalism is like the first model. It is the building of the fence or the wall. There are contexts where that is needed but there are contexts where it doesn't work. However, what if we were to change the focus we had? What if it wasn't about keeping the right 'cows' in and the wrong ones out? What if it was about life? Making sure that we don't stray far away from where the life is. Wouldn't that be a different model?

You see, these fences and walls can often be expressed as cultures or rules. They can exist within nations or families, workplaces or churches. Sometimes those cultural rules are about keeping things the way they 'should be'. If you want to be part of this family, then you have to play by these rules. If you want to get ahead in the workplace, then you need to follow this culture. If you want to live in this country, then you have to be from here. Every time these phrases are uttered it is the sound of another stake in that fence being hammered in or another stone in the wall being slotted into place.

But what if our nations or families or workplaces or churches were more about staying where the life is? What if it wasn't about us and them but about life for all?

What if they weren't tribes but places to belong?

Does Tribalism Scratch Our Itch?

There are many other ways we can see that tribalism is at the centre of our culture and life today. The question is, if tribalism is on the rise, why are we still so dissatisfied? What is missing? Even when we scratch the itch of tribalism, why do we burn for something else?

Is our longing greater than for the tribal factions that we see around us? For a deeper connection: to belong?

I have spent periods of my life searching for where I belong. When I was a child, I learned very quickly that the world was a much better and safer place if you were what people wanted you to be. Through a traumatic loss at a young age, I developed the tendency to try to keep people happy, thinking (often subconsciously) that this would mean they wouldn't leave. As a child, those coping mechanisms aren't as harmful as they are when you are an adult. What it led to, for me, was a profound sense of not knowing who I was. I remember very clearly a conversation in my late teens with my good friend Jon who, as we were walking down the road talking, came out with, 'I don't really know who you are.' What a thing to hear. And yet it changed the way I thought about myself. Did I have to keep on being what people wanted me to be or could I try to find something of myself – whoever that was?

I desperately wanted to fit in, to belong. The strange thing was that I came from a loving family, I was part of a vibrant church, I was in a small school, I had good friends . . . but there was still something missing. That itch was being scratched, but I was still restless.

Really, as I think back over my childhood and my early adulthood, I was on a journey of discovering where I belonged and on a journey to find a deeper sense of belonging than just the tribes I was in. Toko-pa Turner describes it like this:

> The longing to belong is the great silent motivator behind so many of our other ambitions.[11]

So many of the relationships I had, the things I said and did, how I dressed, the music I listened to, were motivated by that simple and yet ancient drive to belong. In the end it was recognizing that this was a 'false self' that I needed to put off in order to go searching for a true self. According to James Martin, SJ:

> The false self is the person that we present to the world, the one that we think will be pleasing to others: attractive, confident, successful. The true self, on the other hand, is the person that we are before God.[12]

That, in a nutshell, has been the journey I have been on. Learning to put off the false self and to put on the true self. It is a journey I am still on because I have to make that decision in dozens of different choices every single day. We all do. Why do we do it? What drives us? The psalmist uses the phrase 'deep calls to deep'.[13]

There is something deeper calling the deeper parts in us, where the true self lives under all the false self we clothe ourselves with. In those hidden depths of us, the depth of God calls to us, stirring the waters of creation and transformation again. We don't always notice; we rarely ever know what the process will look like, but something in us has to answer the call because we know that we weren't made to settle for just scratching the itch.

How many people around the world today, whatever 'tribe' they might feel they are part of, have that drive, that longing for something deeper? How many in our families, our friendships, our workplaces, our schools have that longing? Do you?

And yet so much of what we do, how we try to satisfy that longing in our lives, fits so poorly and fades so quickly and never really does anything more than scratch the itch. In his book *No Man Is An Island*, Thomas Merton challenges us:

> Why do we spend our lives striving to be something we would never want to be, if we only knew what we wanted? Why do we waste our time doing things which, if we only stopped to think about them, are just the opposite of what we were made for?[14]

Does that resonate with you today? Or as you look back over your journey to this point? It certainly does for me. Are you asking these questions around the fire: Where have I come from? Where am I going? Where do I belong? If that is you, then I hope that this book will create some space and opportunity to explore some of those questions.

But I also wanted to encourage you that you are not alone. Countless others around the world are asking these questions, searching for answers. In many ways, it has been the great migration of humanity, to journey on in self-discovery towards home. As I heard someone say recently, 'We are all just walking each other home.'

The words of Merton are a challenge to us as we begin that journey together: 'We are warmed by the fire, not by the smoke of the fire. So too, what we are is to be sought in the invisible depths of our own being . . .'[15]

The deep is calling . . .

2

What Happens When We Don't Belong?

'We don't always get to return home, and not everyone has experienced safe places of belonging.'[1]

Having looked at how tribalism is really an attempt to satisfy the much deeper longing to belong and having identified that search for belonging as the journey deeper which we are all on, there is a big question that we need to explore as we begin that journey.

What happens when we don't belong?

In the same way that each of us will have differing and unique experiences of belonging, we will equally have differing and unique experiences of unbelonging. These experiences are deeply rooted in our personal history and can shape everything we see in the world around us. We might have grown up within a family with very similar experiences as others in the group and yet come out of that family with a very different understanding and feeling of belonging. In that sense, your story is unique but I am hoping that, as we explore this together, there will be points in which you can identify something of yourself.

Getting What You Need

Several years ago I achieved a diploma in CBT,[2] a form of counselling which is used to help people to change the way they think or behave around a certain issue, or in certain circumstances, so that they can manage their problems. It was a fascinating course and one which gave me some really good insight into some basic psychology and how we function as people.

One of the key concepts that stood out to me was called 'the hierarchy of needs' based around the work done by Abraham Maslow in the 1940s. We all have needs as human beings, and these needs vary in importance and scope. What Maslow did was to arrange these needs in a pyramid. The base of the needs that are most important, foundational, are at the bottom of the pyramid, and the other needs are built upon this, a layer at a time. You need each layer to be secure before you can have what is on the next level. Maslow basically categorized his hierarchy of needs like this:

Physiological needs: At the bottom of the pyramid are basic needs such as air, water, food, shelter, sleep and clothing. These were the needs that Maslow thought were most important to the human person and that, without these needs, the human being cannot function properly.

Safety needs: Sitting on top of the physiological needs are ones focused on safety. Needs such as protection from the elements, security, order, law, stability.

Love and belonging needs: This is where Maslow's theory becomes especially relevant for the conversation we are having.

Friendship, intimacy, family and a sense of connection are all needs that fit within this category. According to Maslow, it isn't possible to meet these needs well unless you have the solid foundation of the physiological and the safety needs met below them. That will become especially relevant as we move higher up this pyramid. There are things that keep us alive, that meet our fundamental needs as people, and without which we would die; but according to Maslow, aside from those things, belonging is our deepest need, and on top of a foundation of belonging is built who we are as individuals.

Esteem needs: Here we have respect, self-esteem, status, recognition, strength and freedom.

Self-actualization needs: On top of the pyramid are needs like realizing personal potential, self-fulfilment, seeking personal growth and peak experiences. Essentially, this is about how we have within us a desire to be the best we are capable of becoming.

What is interesting about Maslow's theory in our discussion is that without the need to belong being satisfied, we cannot easily grow and develop as people. Our esteem and self-actualized needs cannot be met unless we have that rooted sense of belonging.

What does it feel like when we don't belong? Like the pyramid has come crashing down on top of you. It can mean low self-esteem, a lack of self-respect and a diminished sense of power and freedom. It can mean that we fail to grow and achieve our full potential.

Belonging, according to Maslow, is not a destination but a foundation on which to build personhood. Weaken or remove it, and everything else tumbles down.

Separated from the Pack

'Like many other pack hunters, humans are guarded and suspicious of difference.'[3]

As I mentioned in the last chapter, being part of a pack is hugely important for many animals as well as human beings.

There are many different 'pack structures', or communities, in our lives. Families, friendship groups, faith communities, workplaces, social groups. Each of these places can be a source of strength and enrichment, but they can also be places which can feel imprisoning and hurtful.

If there is this natural drive within us to be part of the group, to belong, then why do people find themselves on the outside, separated from the pack?

There seem to be two reasons.

Because the pack has excluded them

How painful it is when the community in which you find a sense of belonging and identity chooses to exclude you. This can be especially painful if it is a family community and it is the people whose role it is, of all the people in the world, to care for, protect and nurture you. Perhaps it is that you are different to the rest of your group and that they never quite got you, that it seemed easier for them to not have to deal with that difference and to simply cut you off or, if not completely cut you off, keep you at a distance.

Let me give you a fairly minor example. Many years ago, before I trained to be a minister, I worked for an insurance company. During my time there, I had an accident where I knocked my head and had to have a trip to hospital. I was signed off for a period of time, and even when I went back to work to collect something during my period off, they didn't really want me to be there because I was meant to be at home.

Fast forward a few months. I was told that I was being reprimanded because I had breached financial services protocols on a phone call. I went with a representative from human resources to the meeting, only to be told that I was being fired on the spot. No verbal or written warning. Gone.

When I went home, and the shock had passed, I noticed that the date of the telephone call was a strange one: May 19. I had not been at work. I know this for two reasons. Firstly, because it was my brother-in-law's birthday and I had seen him that day. Secondly, because it was during the period when I was signed off work and the company had not been happy for me to be in the building.

When I appealed the decision with the company managers, it turned out that my line manager, who did not like me, had fabricated the entire thing simply to get rid of me. I was offered my job back, which I politely refused. She lost her job.

I use this as an example because, even though I didn't love my job, it was a painful experience to be excluded in this extreme way. It actually took a couple of years for the internal turbulence to settle and, for a time, whenever I thought about that situation it made me feel angry. Was it the injustice of being wrongfully accused? Perhaps. However, it was certainly about the feeling of being rejected. It is interesting that even a rejection from a group of people you do not know well, in a context you don't really like, can cause so much internal struggle.

Now I could and did get another job. But what happens when you are excluded from a group and you can't move on? What happens when you are excluded from a family group, rejected or misunderstood by that most intimate of packs, but you are still part of the family. Perhaps you have to see them because you still live at home or out of a sense of duty. That's like being fired from the company but you can't even leave the office. Every time you see them, or interact with them, the hurt is just compounded, the hope slowly suffocated and a sense of who you are gradually eradicated with every visit.

No wonder that, in this situation, we have a struggle to find a sense of belonging. It can lead to a sense of disorientation that keeps your head and heart spinning because the one place that was meant to ground you has become the one place where you feel most in flux. As Turner puts it:

> It is the excruciating belief that you are not needed. That life does not consider you necessary.[4]

In a moment, we'll explore some of the issues that might come out of this, but before we do, let's think for a moment about the second reason you might find yourself on the outside of the pack.

Because you choose to leave

What happens when the place of nurture becomes a toxic space? What happens when those bonds of community within the pack become cords that strangle the life from you? What happens when, rather than bathing in that space of belonging, you are drowning in a pit of belonging? What do you do? What are your choices?

You could stick it out. You could make the decision that this group or person is worth staying and fighting for, that change may come. And it might. But, at the same time, we need to make sure that we pay attention and trust the voice within us that seeks to protect and preserve us.

We often as Christians misunderstand 1 Corinthians 10:13: 'God is faithful, and he will not let you be tested beyond your strength . . .'[5]

People have sometimes quoted that verse to me when I have been going through difficult times. To start with, I think the verse is offered out of context. Patrick Regan highlights the challenge with this verse in his helpful book *Honesty Over Silence*:

> It implies that He's the one doling out the pain, and will push
> you right to your limit but then stop right before you crack.[6]

Not only does this distort our view of God during these difficult times, but it gives me a false view of what God believes I should and can handle. It has made me think that if God does not give me situations I cannot handle, then I *must* be able to keep handling them and keep on pushing through them.

Like so many verses in the Bible, we stop the quote before we get the whole picture: '. . . but with the testing he will also provide the way out so that you may be able to endure it.'[7]

So there is a way out so that you can endure.

Sometimes staying is where you start to lose yourself. Because of who you have to become, the mask you have to wear or the wall you have to put up, to be in that situation just breaks you inside: 'The rift is being torn between who you really are, and who you had to be to survive.'[8]

If you are part of a pack or a community where you just don't belong, and that sense of unbelonging is robbing the life from you, know that this is not the best that God has for you. Know that his desire is for you to flourish and grow, to be loved and nurtured and to thrive. Perhaps the healthiest and most life-giving thing to do in a pack where you don't belong, or when belonging isn't healthy or may even be toxic, is to leave. Perhaps that's the way out he's given so that you can endure.

So what can this state of unbelonging look like?

Well it can express itself in our lives in different ways.

Loneliness

Have you ever been in the middle of a crowded room and yet felt alone?

There is a common misunderstanding that loneliness has to do with the number of people around you, and that, as long as there are people around you, then you couldn't possibly be lonely. I know that this is not true because I have stood in those rooms full of people and felt alone.

If belonging is living within that space where we can freely receive and freely give, then loneliness is what happens as a result of one of those channels being blocked. It may be that you have received love, but there is no one you feel you can give that love to. It may be that you have those in your life that you can give love to, but you feel as though you haven't received the love you need in order for it to flow out from you. What results from this is what we call loneliness, the feeling of being trapped in yourself.

Loneliness is on the rise, both in the UK and globally. According to a survey by Age UK in 2018,[9] the number of over 50s in the UK experiencing loneliness is set to reach two million by 2025/26; in 2016/17 it was around 1.4 million. That's an increase of 49 per cent in a decade.

During a time when we are supposed to be more connected than ever before, where we can literally reach out to more people, in more places, than at any other time in our human history, why is it that loneliness is on the rise? Why is it that more and more people are struggling to belong? Even as tribalism is on the rise in our society, our disconnection is rising too, which should tell us something important about tribalism and its mind-set; that it simply is not delivering what so many people need in our world today. At best, it scratches an itch or gives us a sense of fulfilment which doesn't last because it wasn't meant to. There is something deep in the human soul, in the very identity of who we are, which can only be satisfied through belonging, and when we don't experience that, what we are often left with is loneliness.

Loneliness is a condition that can affect people of any age. In March 2017, the charity Relate released some research on the state of our relationships in the UK. In the report called 'You're Not Alone'[10] they presented findings from having surveyed 5,000 people from across the country with some really interesting and troubling findings.

When speaking to young people aged between 17 and 24 about loneliness, 65 per cent of those surveyed said that they felt lonely some of the time. That in itself should be a troubling statistic for a generation so connected by technology and social media. What is even more painful to read is that 32 per cent in that same category said they felt lonely often or all of the time.

One of the contributing factors when it comes to loneliness, especially among young people, is a discrepancy between expectation and reality. We all have expectations in life or of the people around us and ourselves. We have expectations about what our relationships should look like and how we should feel because of them. In itself, this isn't a bad thing although it is good from time to time to take a moment and reflect on how healthy and realistic your expectations are. These expectations are challenging when they are not lived out in the reality of our day-to-day lives.

Let me give you an example with Facebook. I have almost 100 friends on Facebook, which I think is probably a little lower than average. Of those 100 friends, I have probably interacted in the past six months with about 50 per cent of them on Facebook itself and probably only 25 per cent in the 'real world'. I have posted forty times in the last six months and have averaged 1.25 comments per post. So, on average, less than 2 per cent of my friends on Facebook are commenting on what I'm posting. This is in no way a criticism of my Facebook community because I'm not a great one for commenting on other people's posts, but it is to highlight that sometimes reality doesn't meet your expectation. My expectation, realistic or not, is that more of my friends would comment on my posts; the reality is that they don't. And that can and does leave me with a sense of loneliness at times. There are times when I have come off Facebook because of it. Perhaps this should lead us to think about the balance between our expectations and reality. Is there an imbalance here which is causing you to feel as though you aren't belonging? Maybe it's manifesting itself in loneliness, but the root feeling is that we simply don't belong.

What this highlights, though, is another issue. Perhaps there are sizes of community where that sense of belonging is just harder to maintain and loneliness is more likely.

For three years when I was training for ministry, we lived in south-east London. Growing up in a small overspill town in Hampshire with a population of 30,000 was not much of an adequate preparation for living in a city of 9 million people.

That said, it was a fantastic three years with some wonderful people and amazing memories and we always enjoy going back to London. We recently went back for my birthday and took Leo to see the dinosaurs at the Natural History Museum and I was struck again just by the sheer number of people who live in the city.

I was having a conversation recently with my friend and colleague Dave, and he highlighted this very important point about the size of a community and the ability for people to respond to and connect with each other within it. If you live in a little hamlet and there are four other people there, the odds are that you will know those four people fairly well because they are the only people that you have to speak to and engage with. The size of the community enables there to be good opportunity to form relationships that connect and foster a sense of belonging. In a city of 9 million people, there are just too many to do this with, and so very often, people walk through the city, or travel through the city, and don't speak or connect with another person. That used to be my joke when I lived in London: that, if you said 'good morning' to someone on the street, they would assume that you were about to attack them or there was something wrong with you. There are just some places which are too big for this connection to meaningfully take place.

Think again about Facebook. At its best, it is a way to get information from lots of people you know, all in one place at any time of the day. It is like a magic mirror into the lives of your friends. What it is not – however it is billed – is a means to genuinely connect with people, build relationships or foster a sense of belonging. It is just too big for that.

What happens, though, when you have 100 friends that you just can't connect with? You get lonely. You feel isolated. You withdraw. You are in a virtual room with hundreds, but it feels like you've been unplugged from the matrix. The real world seems a lot more threatening.

In terms of the effect that loneliness has on us as human beings, it ranges from mental health issues to physical problems such as dementia and heart disease. A study by Julianne Holt-Lunstad in 2010 found that loneliness is likely to increase a person's risk of death by 29 per cent and can be as bad for your health as smoking 15 cigarettes a day.[11] It is endemic in our modern society, and we cannot simply ignore it anymore.

We each have a need to be recognized. God has created us as human beings to be born into relationship. It is reflected in the relationship between the first human beings, and it has been a feature of our lives ever since. Part of the way we see ourselves is through the eyes of others, and in the recognition of others, we find a degree of stability – if that recognition is accepting and healthy.

If relationship is part of God's good plan for us and can form a positive core at the centre of who we are as human beings, if we are made to belong, then a lack of belonging can only come about when things like rejection, loneliness, a lack of care and acceptance drive us from that relational space.

The Broken Pot

There is another result of a lack of belonging which we haven't touched on yet, but is a very common and painful one: shame.

We saw at the beginning of the chapter, when we looked at Maslow's hierarchy of needs, that, if we do not have a sense of belonging, then it is very difficult to have a secure sense of self. Self-esteem can be badly affected by the rejection that comes from feeling that you don't belong. That lack of self-esteem can then cause the very damaging state of shame to exist within a person.

Shame is a complex emotional state which will vary from person to person, but it can lead to a place where a person experiencing bad situations thinks it is because they themselves are bad.

It's important here to differentiate between guilt and shame. Guilt is an acknowledgment that you have done something wrong; shame is a belief that you yourself are bad. Guilt is about behaviour; shame is about identity.

Perhaps one of the roots of this attitude of shame is the rejection that is experienced by a person and the message that it sends to them that they are the problem. This script goes round and round in a person's mind to the point where they accept that everything bad that happens to them or around them must be because there is something wrong with them.

This mind-set can lead to, or be fed by, perfectionism – that, if I manage to get everything right or perfect, then I will be acceptable or, at least, it will hide the imperfect me.

Shame is not just a product of our lack of belonging; it can be a barrier to belonging, too, because we feel as though we are not worthy of acceptance.

Let us think about this in the framework of a story Jesus told:

Then Jesus said, 'There was a man who had two sons. The younger of them said to his father, "Father, give me the share of the property that will belong to me." So he divided his property between them. A few days later the younger son gathered all he had and travelled to a distant country, and there he squandered his property in dissolute living. When he had spent everything, a severe famine took place throughout that country, and he began to be in need. So he went and hired himself out to one of the citizens of that country, who sent him to his fields to feed the pigs. He would gladly have filled himself with the pods that the pigs were eating; and no one gave him anything. But when he came to himself he said, "How many of my father's hired hands have bread enough and to spare, but here I am dying of hunger! I will get up and go to my father, and I will say to him, 'Father, I have sinned against heaven and before you; I am no longer worthy to be called your son; treat me like one of your hired hands.'" So he set off and went to his father. But while he was still far off, his father saw him and was filled with compassion; he ran and put his arms around him and kissed him. Then the son said to him, "Father, I have sinned against heaven and before you; I am no longer worthy to be called your son." But the father said to his slaves, "Quickly, bring out a robe – the best one – and put it on him; put a ring on his finger and sandals on his feet. And get the fatted calf and kill it, and let us eat and celebrate; for this son of mine was dead and is alive again; he was lost and is found!" And they began to celebrate.'[12]

The son has left the father and lived his wild life in the far away city. However, when the money runs out and his 'friends' abandon him, he realizes that life can be harsher than he ever thought possible. There, in the muck and the dirt, surrounded by the stench of the pigs, the young man has a realization. Note what the son says: 'Father, I have sinned against heaven and before you . . .'[13]

This is guilt. It is about his behaviour. He has acted in a way – the word he uses is 'sin' – which has broken the relationship between him and the father. It has taken him outside of the space of belonging and family. He feels the weight of it.

But look at where he goes next: 'I am no longer worthy to be called your son; treat me like one of your hired hands.'[14]

This is shame. This is about identity. Listen to his words: 'I am no longer worthy.'

We see the difference between guilt and shame here in the first few words of each verse.

Verse 18 is guilt: 'I *have* . . .'

Verse 19 is shame: 'I *am* . . .'

That shame is one which he feels takes him forever outside of the space of belonging. He is content, because of his sense of shame, to relinquish his identity as the son. Here, in the muck, he feels anything but the son of his father. He is content to be a servant.

There is a hopelessness in the language of the son here. Regardless of what he has done, whether he is the architect of his own situation or not, many who have been in a place of shame can identify with his words here. 'Shame feels hopeless: that no matter what we do, we cannot correct it. We feel isolated and lonely with our shame . . .'[15]

Now look at verse 20:

So he set off and went to his father. But while he was still far off, his father saw him and was filled with compassion; he ran and put his arms around him and kissed him.[16]

There has been much written about the fact that the father runs. For many people, this parable isn't called the parable of the prodigal son but the parable of the running father. Fathers in the culture where Jesus tells this story did not run. It was seen as an undignified thing to do because, to do it, the father would have to have hitched up his robes to stop from tripping over. So it would have been a shocking thing for the father to do. It says a lot about the father in the parable that 'in a culture where senior figures are far too dignified to run anywhere, this man takes to his heels as soon as he sees his young son dragging himself home'.[17]

Aside from the father running to meet the son because of his love for him, perhaps there was another reason which links in with what we are discussing here about shame. It has its meaning in the historical and cultural roots of the time Jesus lived.

When a son, in the time of Jesus, left his family and brought dishonour on his family and community, on his return they would meet him at the limits of the city and perform the *kezazah* ceremony.[18] This was a shame ceremony in which the community would smash a large pot at the feet of the son, symbolically showing the broken and irreparable relationship between them. He was now cut off. He did not belong. His shame was complete.

So perhaps this is why the father runs to meet the son. The father takes on the shame of running in order to spare his son the shame of this ceremony. As the parable is to illustrate a deeper truth, so God (the father) takes on our (the son) shame in order to save us from it. Notice that in the parable the son is always referred to as 'son'. Six times in our passage he is mentioned as the son, the majority of times after he has squandered his inheritance. Whatever his actions, his identity has not changed. He is kept within this space of belonging, not because of his own actions but because of the father who will not let the shame of his son be the defining characteristic of the relationship. He brings him in. He restores him. He celebrates his presence.

The same that is true for the prodigal is true for you and me, too. Whatever you feel has been the cause of your shame, loneliness or lack of belonging, know that this is not how God sees you. If you feel as though something is broken within you, know that he looks on you with love. If you feel as though there is nothing good in you because you believe that you aren't good, know that he looks on you as worthy. Because he loves you and never once on the long and winding road of your life have you ever stopped being anything other than his child.

The feelings we have explored in this chapter are painful and complex. The few that I have touched on, I have only touched on briefly. It may be that you need support to journey through some of these issues, so let me encourage you to get the support that you need. There have been times in my life where I have needed to work through and process hurts from the past, and while that has never been easy, I can promise you that it will be worth it in the end.

In the coming chapters, we will explore some areas of belonging and what that might look like for us as people who are made to belong.

3

Belonging to Yourself

*'Our sense of belonging can never be greater than
our level of self-acceptance.'*[1]

I was born in Poole in the UK on Wednesday 1 February 1984
to parents Sue and David Ferneyhough. My sister Hannah
was born fifteen months later and, after a few little moves, we
moved into a road near the church we were attending as a family in September 1987. Despite ill health stopping my parents
from being medical missionaries in Papua New Guinea, my father had started work as the associate pastor at Andover Baptist
Church and had begun his theological training. Dark clouds
were forming and just one short month later, in October 1987,
my father suffered a massive stroke and died leaving my mother
as a thirty-year-old single parent of two children under the age
of four. It also left Hannah and me without a father.

I am so thankful for family and friends, as well as the church
community, who were around us in the days after my father
died. I was of course too young to remember but, in little
pieces of the story I have picked up over the years, I know now
just what a support structure we had around us.

And, of course, my mum. I don't think you can appreciate
it until you are older, but my mum loved and cared and did

her best for us as children, even in the middle of her own grief and loss. I read recently that 'single parenting is parenting for marines',[2] and if that's true, then my mum has well earned her green beret.

I also am very blessed to see the impact and example of a mother's love by the beautiful, selfless and life-giving way that my wife, Bex, parents our son Leo. So I know the significance that this love has on a young life from two first-hand experiences.

My story doesn't stay in that place. In 1989, my mum met Brian (Dad), and in June 1991 they were married. I remember reading that 'it takes a special person to be open to being with someone who has loved and lost at such a deep level'[3] and that is certainly true of my dad.

Grace came along in March 1992 and this new family of five was complete.

I'll talk a little bit more about family dynamics in the next chapter, but there is a unique consequence of my family situation which can highlight what we are looking at in this chapter.

When he married my mum, Dad didn't legally adopt us. He wanted that to be our choice and, at the age of seven and six, we weren't old enough to make that choice. So I grew up and went to primary school as Andrew Ferneyhough. I remember wanting to take on my dad's surname, Percey, and we talked about how that might happen. I remember where I was when I told my parents that I wanted to change my name. We were on holiday in France at the time, and all I remember was that we were walking alongside a river, and I think it was on the bridge over the river that I brought it up. I think I might have been nine or ten years old.

The challenge was that, when you legally change your name, you have to officially renounce your previous name, and we didn't feel that this was something that I should do. So the compromise was that I would simply be known as Andrew Percey. When I started secondary school, that was what happened. I applied and was accepted as Andrew Percey. At that moment, Andrew Ferneyhough dropped off the face of the planet, and out of nowhere, Andrew Percey appeared. There was no legal basis to this name; it was essentially an alias. This carried on perfectly well all the way through secondary school, and we only became aware of the tension this provided when I reached the age of sixteen, but it came through an unusual turn of events.

During the summer of the year 2000, after I had finished secondary school, my good friend Jon and I spent several weeks visiting Malawi. There was a missionary couple from the church serving there, and Jon and I were going to stay with them. It was an amazing opportunity for two sixteen-year-old boys to see something of the world that was totally removed from what we had experienced before. At the time, Malawi was the third poorest country in the world and, having grown up in Test Valley in the central south of the UK, nothing could really have prepared us for it.

I booked my ticket with money that I had saved for months (ironically in Bath Travel – where I now live) under the name Andrew Percey. It was the name I had used for the five years previously, the name I had my GCSE qualifications in and even a bank account. Some of you may be able to see what was coming. Nearer to the time, we realized that my passport did not have the same name as my ticket. To change the ticket would have been expensive, so we investigated whether it was possible to change the name on my passport. After some long conversations and having been referred to the head of the passport office, the passport was changed.

I went to Malawi and had an incredible time, which still stays with me to this day, twenty years on. When I got back, however, we were contacted again by the passport office to say that there had been a mistake, and the passport should not have been issued. They had given me a passport for a name that didn't technically exist. I was 'known as' Andrew Percey, but was legally Andrew Ferneyhough, and they had given me a legal form of identity for a name that was an alias. There was nothing that they could do to correct the problem and had, in effect, accidentally given me dual identity. At the time, I was the only person in the country who wasn't in witness protection to have it.

That situation continues to this day. What it has always meant is that for me the issue of belonging to myself seems far more complex than it might have otherwise done. I am legally two different people.

In this chapter, I want us to explore what it means to belong to ourselves; to own our own stories and to feel at home in who we are. If we struggle with this then I think there will be other areas in our lives that we will struggle to belong to as well.

Know Yourself

Since our True Self went into hiding and our False Self then had to run the show, it may be hard to know who we really are.[4]

I ended the first chapter of the book by speaking about the 'true self' and the 'false self'. When it comes to a conversation about how we know who we are, then this language can be a real help to us.

There is automatically a problem though. It is often much easier for us to know 'who we are not' than it is to know 'who we are'. The things that we sometimes say and do, or the way we sometimes feel, can grate internally. We just know instinctively that this is not who we are. That this is not who we were created to be. That we are not operating, in those moments, in line with our true self. But what is the true self?

There has been some discussion among psychologists about whether the true self is static or evolving. Is it something deep and unchangeable at the core of who I am as a person? Or is it the process I am going through in order to become who I really am? In many ways the answer is both. At the core of who you are is a very important and unchanging truth that, when we realize it, can give us both the safe home of acceptance, and the outward travel of transformation. Here it is: 'You have been created in love, to be loved.'

It might not sound like much, and you might not be surprised by it. However, when we not only grasp this truth but live it out, then, not only will we be operating out of the core of who we are, but we will be growing into a fuller reflection of that truth as well.

Personality grows all the time. We are on a seemingly unending quest of discovering more about who we are, what we like and dislike and how we respond to certain circumstances. Those aspects of us change from person to person and that is a reflection of the amazing diversity that God has created the world to reflect. You were not made to be like anyone else. You are not meant to be like anyone else. You were made to be you. Fully, freely and authentically you. It is important that you learn to become aware of the parts of you that are unique. The preferences and the desires and the gifts that you have and how you can express them in a way that brings you life.

Self-awareness is a largely under-rated quality. So many people, even some within our families and communities, do not ask the questions that take them deep within themselves, and because of this, they miss out on discovering who they are. Rather than living in response to who we are, we become simply reactive, responding instinctively to what is going on around us rather than taking hold of a situation and responding to it out of a place of internal security.

Thousands of years ago, the psalmist wrote:

> For you created my innermost parts, wove me in my mother's womb. I acclaim you, for awesomely I am set apart, wondrous are your acts, and my being deeply knows it.[5]

I love the depth and beauty of Robert Alter's translation. What he points out in this passage is that there is evidence to translate, as we usually do, 'fearfully and wonderfully made', as 'awesomely I am set apart'. Alter reflects:

> That meaning might be appropriate for the speaker's reflection on how he evolved in the womb from an unformed embryo to a particular human being with the consciousness of his own individuality.[6]

What does it mean to be fearfully and wonderfully made or to be awesomely set apart? That, in the whole course of human history, in the billions who have come before and yet more billions to come, there has never been anyone like you. That you are unique. You are precious. That God has shaped a little bit of his image and likeness into the shape of you.

How does Alter continue? 'My being deeply knows it.' That, deep down inside of us, we know who we are. We might not always be able to consciously recall, and that is the great challenge, but it does not make it less true.

Some of the blocks that help us to connect with that deep knowing of our identity in God are written into our very theology. In a previous church, we spent some time reworking our statement of faith, which was both a long and painful process. I think in the end it took almost a year, and we had some very late-night meetings and some heated discussions about the nature of what we believe. One of the main sticking points was on the nature of humanity. The church's historic statement of faith spoke about the fallen nature of human beings, about depravity and sin. In essence, it was the doctrine of original sin, which goes all the way back to Augustine in the fourth century. It is the belief that we are each born sinful and that our nature is essentially shaped by that until we are saved. It seems to have been at the heart of what many have believed about human nature. The challenge when we came to that was some of us could see what this statement was trying to say, but it was the wrong starting point for the conversation.

For me, as I reflect on the Scriptures and as I think about how Jesus came alongside those who were struggling with the weight of their own mistakes, I would like to start the conversation in a different place.

We are created in love, to be loved. That is how we are created. As John reflects in one of his short letters at the end of the New Testament: 'See what love the Father has given us, that we should be called children of God; and that is what we are.'[7]

Yes sin, however we want to define that, has corrupted the world in which we live and has muddied the waters of our knowing who we are as children of God, often driving a wedge between us. But to say that this is who we are in our very nature, I think, causes more harm than good.

According to J. Philip Newell, it is in helping us to know this deep truth of who we are that Christ's ministry was rooted. He reflects on the gospel as good news, and challenges the view point that our 'fallen-ness' is either 'news' or 'good'.[8] We know that we make mistakes and we see the damage that it causes. Newell writes:

> So the gospel is not given to tell us what we already know. Rather, the gospel is given to tell us what we do not know or what we have forgotten, and that is who we are, sons and daughters of the One from whom all things come.[9]

So Jesus comes to remind us of who we are, to help us to know who we are and to teach us to belong within that part of ourselves that is created and rooted in our beloved-ness.

Yes, the circumstances of life and of sin can cause damage to that identity and image, but this is where the spirit of God as the being of grace comes to help us to live again within that truth.

Belonging to myself is a journey I go on to be reminded of the reality of who I am as someone created in love, to be loved. The journey, though, is not about changing me to be something different, because this is who I am. Rather it is about stripping away all the things I am not. This is not easy. The infection of all those false identities and the cancer of sin is deep within our humanity and there are times when it needs to be drastically and skilfully cut out. Recovery can be long and painful.

However, that infection is not who we are – in the same way that a cancer patient is not defined merely by their illness. At the risk of repeating myself, we are the ones created in love, to be loved. Paul's great prayer to the Ephesians makes it clear to us:

> I pray that you may have the power to comprehend, with all the saints, what is the breadth and length and height and depth, and **to know the love of Christ** that surpasses knowledge, so that you may be filled with all the fullness of God.[10]

Love Yourself

In Matthew 22, Jesus is asked about what the greatest commandment is:

> When the Pharisees heard that he had silenced the Sadducees, they gathered together, and one of them, a lawyer, asked him a question to test him. 'Teacher, which commandment in the law is the greatest?' He said to him, '"You shall love the Lord your God with all your heart, and with all your soul, and with all your mind." This is the greatest and first commandment. And a second is like it: "You shall love your neighbour as yourself." On these two commandments hang all the law and the prophets.'[11]

Love God. Love your neighbour. Or love God and love others. These are the two reflections on this passage that I hear most often. Yet there is a third that many miss, and it's important for our conversation about belonging to yourself – love yourself! It's those two little words at the end of verse 39 that often we find hardest to do: 'as yourself'.

We often get trapped in believing that we do not have worth and value. And, if we do not have worth and value, then it is really hard to love ourselves. If it is hard to love ourselves, then it is really hard to love others: 'Once we begin to see ourselves as "worthless," "un-loveable," "undesirable," or "unacceptable," we tend to get wedged into that space.'[12]

Love makes the world go round. As Gary Chapman wrote in his popular book *The Five Love Languages*:

> Psychologists have concluded that the need to feel loved is a primary human emotional need. For love we will climb

mountains, cross seas, traverse desert sands, and endure untold hardships. Without love, mountains become unclimbable, seas uncrossable, deserts unbearable and hardships our lot in life.[13]

I know that I have been in that space. Where I have felt as though there was nothing to love in me. When I looked deep down inside and just felt dirty and worthless, as though I had extinguished any light in me or polluted any goodness. That I was all too aware of my faults and the mistakes I had made. The mountains seemed to be unclimbable and the seas uncrossable. I was trapped in the desert of my own lack of self-love, unable to hear the cries of affirmation from those around me, unable to hear the voice of my loving heavenly Father.

It took several years and many tears to be loved back into that place. I had lots of counselling and had to learn not to be ashamed to seek help when that help was so desperately needed. I was blessed in that I have an amazing wife who literally loved me back to life and health.

Why is it important to love yourself? Well, that might seem like a strange question to ask, but many people find it a complicated one or at least a difficult thing to live out in the reality of their lives. We've already explored that we are created in love, that we are precious and valuable. It is that worth that comes from the very core of our being that gives us the platform to love ourselves and then to love others as a result.

If I have a £10 note in my wallet and I screw it up into a tiny ball in my fist so it is crumpled and not as pristine as it first was, does the value of the note change? No, of course not. If I drop it on the floor and stamp on it, making it dirty and dusty, does it stop being worth £10? No. Because the value is not based on the condition of the note; it is based on a promise and a guarantee. The next time you look at a £10 note you will see written on it: 'I promise to pay the bearer on demand the sum of ten pounds'.

The promise is what keeps the value of the note, and that promise, should we ever doubt it, is guaranteed by the Bank of England, who make the notes. You have value and worth, you are precious and treasured, you are loved. The condition you are in does not change that. You might feel as though you've been crushed and crumpled by life; your value does not change! You might feel as though you have been stamped and trodden on by others; your value does not change! Why? Because God has promised that this is who you are, in his Word, through his Son. That promise is guaranteed by the One who made you. You are his!

> But now thus says the LORD, he who created you, O Jacob, he who formed you, O Israel: Do not fear, for I have redeemed you; I have called you by name, you are mine. When you pass through the waters, I will be with you; and through the rivers, they shall not overwhelm you; when you walk through fire you shall not be burned, and the flame shall not consume you. For I am the LORD your God, the Holy One of Israel, your Saviour.[14]

God doesn't want us to simply know that he loves us and that we have worth and value in an academic sense. He wants us to live in the reality of that truth. To thrive and enjoy life. To be free to play and embrace the adventure of life as the ones created in love, to be loved. A lack of self-love robs us of that joy. As Joyce Meyer says: 'You are the one person you never get away from. If you don't like yourself, if you don't get along with yourself, you are doomed to misery.'[15] Just as with any parent, that is not what God wants for you.

The difficult aspect of this conversation is that we tend to view how we give and receive love as separate things. As we have already explored, this language of freely giving and receiving is at the heart of belonging. While we might talk about them in different ways, they are part of the same thing. How we love and how we receive love are always flowing in and out of each other, mingling in a thousand tiny interactions and internal conversations each and every day.

We can only give what we have. If I see love as a way of getting a sense of self-validation or as a means of feeling better about myself, then the way I see others will reflect that. People will simply become objects whose attention I seek when I need a boost, or avoid if they make me feel lower.

A common one is if people have a high degree of self-critique. If you are really hard on yourself and only see lots of faults, then you will probably be harsh and critical towards others. If you are uncertain about your worth, then you will probably be uncertain about the worth of others as well.

It comes back to what we were saying earlier in the chapter about the starting point. If the starting point is negative, or not good news, then this is not only the place you will keep coming back to, but it is the default we will easily slip back to when it comes to how we see others as well. It is the mud we get stuck in again and again.

However, if we understand our value and our worth as those created in love, to be loved, then we can start to learn to love ourselves too. We can not only be reminded of that nature but we can start to remind ourselves of it on a regular basis too. Then we will start to see in our interactions with others the love that they give, and we can start to love them from a place of security, even though the love they give isn't perfect.

Patrick Dodson wrote a moving book called *Stuff My Dad Never Told Me About Relationships*, and in the chapter called 'I Love Me' he says:

> We can't love our neighbour unless we love ourselves. We can't communicate our heart and dreams without being really in touch with our identity.[16]

Perhaps a good place to start is using 1 Corinthians 13 as a framework:

> Love is patient; love is kind; love is not envious or boastful or arrogant or rude. It does not insist on its own way; it is not irritable or resentful; it does not rejoice in wrongdoing, but rejoices in the truth. It bears all things, believes all things, hopes all things, endures all things. Love never ends.[17]

What would it look like if we tried to live this out in our lives as an act of self-love?

What if we tried to be patient with ourselves rather than getting caught up with that sense of constant frustration?

What if we were kind to ourselves, realizing that we are simply trying our best with the tools we have?

What if our sense of self wasn't wrapped up in being better than others or comparing ourselves to others? Would that get rid of a need to boast or be envious?

What if we weren't so self-critical? Wouldn't that free us from irritability and resentfulness?

And instead of constantly finding things that prop up a negative view of ourselves – an internal 'rejoicing in wrongdoing' – what if we focused on the truth of who we are as created in love, to be loved – and rejoice in that truth?

What if we bared with ourselves; believed in ourselves; had hope in ourselves?

What if, in our quest to love ourselves, we realized that this love never gives up?

Would that make a difference to our internal conversation? Perhaps that is something we can try to put into practice? Why not use this as a framework, taking one aspect at a time. Why not start at the top with patience? In the coming days and weeks (maybe even months), try to be patient with yourself. Of course there will be times when you become frustrated, but in those moments, try to pause and to remember this verse and say to yourself that you are doing the best that you can.

Another helpful tool is to try to not compare yourself with others. This is really hard, and we live in an age where social media in particular makes it really hard. We are bombarded with images of beautiful people in exotic places doing spectacular things; of smiling, happy and compliant kids; of well-groomed dogs and sunny days. And we think, 'That's not my life', or at least not all the time. 'What's wrong with me?' That's the curse of comparison, and it's one that you can't measure up to, so why not stop trying?

True belonging doesn't require you to change who you are; it requires you to be who you are.[18]

Be you. Unashamedly you. That's who God made you and how he loves you. May your eyes be opened to look at yourself through the eyes of your perfect heavenly parent.

In the chapters to come we will explore a little more of what it means to belong to others. Whether it's the family or church, creation or God, we will begin to look outside ourselves for that sense of connectedness and belonging.

What is important for us to realize, though, is that belonging to ourselves is vitally important and totally linked with how we belong to others. Here we have found a place of grounding, a place we can come back to again and again; and there will be times where we need to do that.

Brené Brown encourages us, 'Once we belong thoroughly to ourselves and believe thoroughly in ourselves, true belonging is ours.'[19]

As you sit by the fire and hear the words of your own story, may you be rooted in the truth that God delights in you, that you have worth and value . . . and may you learn to know and love yourself as the one created in love, to be loved.

4

Thicker than Water?

'Our family is our home; the place where we know we belong.'[1]

How many Christmas dinners do you have? I ask the question partly because the Christmas decorations have started to go up in the supermarkets and the weather is getting more wintery and perhaps my mind is starting to turn towards Christmas. Do you have one big meal? Do you have one meal for your own family and then another with your in-laws? Perhaps you don't have a Christmas meal?

In the previous chapter, I mentioned the family situation I grew up with, which essentially gave me three families. One of the wonderful side effects of that was that I also got to have three Christmas lunches. Not only did I get to enjoy those but I also got to spend three separate occasions celebrating with family, which was a highlight of Christmas.

On Christmas Eve, we went to Nana and Grampy's (my dad's parents). On Christmas Day, we had Mum's side of the family over to our house. On Boxing Day, we went to Nana and Grandad's house (my father's parents).

By the time December 27th came, we didn't have the capacity to go anywhere!

My family situation is not unique (there may be some of you reading this who can identify with what it is to come from a family situation like mine) but neither is it 'normal'. I am aware that we have different experiences even within our own family. For example, my sister Grace and I, while being part of the same family, have different experiences because we have a slightly different history.

Belonging: The Dance That Helps Us to Thrive

When family life is working well and each member of that family feels a sense of belonging, it can be an environment where everyone can thrive. For me, family has been a place of belonging. When I say that, I don't want to give the impression that our family is perfect; it isn't. What I mean is that I grew up with a sense of rootedness to a group of people where I was able to receive and give love freely.

Families aren't static. People change and grow over time, and the circumstances in which families live will change as well. Change is a natural and healthy part of life. In families, there is a paradox in our growing together because the goal is not only to grow closer together but to gain a greater sense of freedom and identity at the same time. When people live within a family environment with a sense of belonging, then not only will they grow closer to members of that family but they will also grow in their own sense of who they are. The aim is not co-dependence but neither is it estrangement.

Growing up, I knew that I was loved. My parents' love wasn't perfect, but I didn't doubt it. I knew that whatever I did, I would be loved. That kind of love gives you a sense of belonging or connection, which can enable you to know yourself and which can lay a positive foundation for who you are into the years ahead.

Family, when it is working well, is also like a dance. Now, I say that to you as someone who, when he dances, looks like a mannequin in an earthquake. In a dance, there needs to be movement, and that movement must be in sync with the others in the dance otherwise the whole thing falls apart. Mark and Lisa Scandrette, co-founders of 'ReImagine' which is a centre for Integral Christian Practice, say, 'A family isn't just a collection of individuals but a dynamic system of relationships.'[2] That dynamic system is one that flows and moves throughout the rhythm of life. Even when one person moves away from the others in the dance, there is an opportunity to find a new movement and expression to the family dynamic. Let me give you an example from the very beginning: 'That is why a man leaves his father and mother and is united to his wife, and they become one flesh.'[3]

The moving together of the husband and the wife is a moving away from the father and the mother. A new family is formed that has to find its way in the world and its own ways of belonging, its own rhythm of the dance. However, there is also an opportunity for the parents, rather than just letting their child slip away, to be part of this new dynamic system by finding their own, and maybe different, place to belong within this new family environment.

The story I grew up with gives me a sense of rootedness and has been a place of belonging, but the place where I most fully and freely find that is in my relationships with my wife and my son. It is here that I most fully give and receive love. It is here that I am most wholly defined and where I experience a whole different level of belonging.

Now, I am aware that for some of you reading this, you may not have children, you may be single or you may not have a family. When I talk about my family, it is not because I believe that the way I have described is better than any other situation. My family situation is exactly that – mine – and yours will be different. The closest family to you may not be the person you are married to. It may be that you have been unable to have children. I hope that in what I share you are able to substitute the examples I use from my own life and make them work for your own situation.

Using the example of Jesus' words 'freely receive, freely give', what does that look like in my family when it is working well? It means, in my marriage, that I am open to receiving from my wife. Not just love, comfort, support and strength but also guidance and correction. That I am not just open to receiving *from* her but that I am open to receiving *her*. All she is, in the good times and the bad times, in sickness and in health, when she gets it right and when she occasionally gets it wrong. After all, that was what I promised her thirteen years ago when we got married. That is what I strive for as a husband. I do not always get it right, but that is what I aim for. But it has to work in the little moments, which is, of course, what life is made up of.

It isn't just about receiving, though, but about giving too: giving her my time, the best of it rather than the dregs of it and giving her my attention. In the same way that I receive *her*, I am giving her *me*; not holding back parts of myself but sharing the real me.

What does that mean in my relationship as a father? Well, many of the same things. Every night when I look at my beautiful son sleeping, I am grateful to God for him. Every single day I tell him that I love him. That I try to give him the best of me, shield him from the worst of me and try to learn, grow and develop as I see how he learns, grows and develops.

It is worth asking: what does it mean to freely receive and freely give within my family?

How can I receive the love that my family have towards me, and how can I give that love in return? When those channels of receiving and giving are open and we are giving ourselves to one another and receiving each other in love, then we are experiencing a strong sense of belonging.

Within any group, including families, people will give and receive love differently. Your family, spouse, children, parents, siblings or other family members will all give and receive love in ways that express who they are. This is why the dance is so important. It enables us to move towards each other and be responsive to each other and they to us. So it is not only helpful to reflect on how you give and receive love within your family but to ask yourself how others in your family need you to give and receive love.

A great dance needs a great rhythm. What is the rhythm in your family? Is there a rhythm or do you find that you are going through life as a family like that mannequin in the earthquake, just shaking about all over the place, from one place to another as the tremors of life take you?

To be part of a great dance, we need a good rhythm, so it's important to compose a rhythm for your family which will give a voice and a space for everyone to belong. Time to rest, to work, to play, to pray. Time to share food and celebrate together. Mark and Lisa Scandrette reflect: 'Rhythms are good habits we create to allow our deepest values to shape the cadence of our lives.'[4]

In their chapter 'A Thriving Family Finds its Rhythm', Mark and Lisa reflect on how they have set a rhythm to their family life that reflects their daily, weekly, monthly and seasonal priorities, values, needs and desires.

Perhaps this is something that you can try within your own family life. Talk about it together so that each member of

the family finds they can contribute in shaping that culture
and rhythm. That again will help to grow the sense of family
belonging.

As I have already mentioned, people, families and situations
change over time. I am not now the same man I was when I
married Bex at the age of twenty-three. Neither am I the same
man I was when our son Leo was born in 2015 because I have
learned to dance with them, and in order to do that, I have had
to change the way I move. They have also changed to dance
with me. You may need to come back to this periodically to
check you are still dancing in step with each other. The important thing is that you do this together so that you get the joy
and honour of belonging to your family. If you make the moves
without them, if you don't do it with them, then you belong
simply to an ideal of what your family should be rather than
who they really are.

Is Blood Thicker Than Water?

Who is my family?

Most of us will be familiar with the phrase 'blood is thicker
than water'. And most will have taken from that the meaning that family relationships are deeper than those outside of
family. Is that really the case? What happens when you are in
a family that is dysfunctional? What happens if you have been
caused real hurt by your family? I'll come to that in a moment.
As I have already said, it may be that the strongest family connections you feel are not with those who you are biologically
related to or from within your own family.

I know within my own church that, on Mother's and Father's
Days, we also celebrate those who have been parental figures in

our lives but who are not our biological parents. I know from several members of my own congregation that this has been significant and valued.

On Father's Day this year, I preached at a friend's church in the evening on the parable of the prodigal son from Luke 15. It is a fascinating story about family and the depths that love will go to in order to reclaim and restore; I'm sure you know the story well. What I shared was that my life had been impacted by three moments of fatherhood.

Firstly, there was the death of my father when I was three years old. My earliest memory of fatherhood was that I didn't have a father. I remember vividly going to school and watching other children go home with their dads and knowing that I couldn't. I can still, over thirty years later, remember doing that. I knew what it was like to grow up in a home where something was missing; some*one* was missing.

Lastly, I spoke about my own experience as a father: how my life has changed in countless ways for the better and my life enriched more than I ever thought possible by this little person being a part of it. That I have a greater glimpse into what it must be for God to parent us, both the joy and the heartache.

In the middle, I spoke about my mum's marriage to my dad in 1991. I started to call him Dad just before they got married. I may not have been legally adopted by my dad but I was adopted into his heart. There is a space there which is just for me. I belong to him and he belongs to me. That bond is not in our biology although it reverberates in the very fibres of who we are. It is a bond that has been forged and earned and nurtured in a thousand little moments spanning decades.

So what about this saying about blood and water? Does that mean that the love my dad and I have for each other is less than the love between a biologically related father and son? Of course not. The only difference is our biology, but in every way that matters, he is my dad.

You may not know, but the saying 'blood is thicker than water' is only part of the famous saying, and it actually means something different to the story we have traditionally told. It comes from an old English proverb which says, 'The blood of the covenant is thicker than the water of the womb.'[5]

The proverb demonstrates the bond that soldiers had standing next to each other, shedding their blood together on the battlefield and how that bond was stronger than the family bond. How often that is true in our family situations too. It is not automatically those who share our biology with whom we have the strongest bonds, but it is those who have stood alongside us, fought for us, protected and served us. It is not those whose blood we share but those who have shed their blood for us in the battlefield moments of life that we can truly say 'we belong to each other'.

What comes to mind in the gospel is the experience of Jesus at the cross:

> Near the cross of Jesus stood his mother, his mother's sister, Mary the wife of Clopas, and Mary Magdalene. When Jesus saw his mother there, and the disciple whom he loved standing nearby, he said to her, 'Woman, here is your son,' and to the disciple, 'Here is your mother.' From that time on, this disciple took her into his home.[6]

Why is it that Jesus chooses John to look after his mother? Perhaps it is because John is there. He is standing with Jesus in this significant battlefield moment of his life, and because of that, the bond between them is essentially family.

And of course this drawing in of others into the family of Jesus is powerfully at the centre of the gospel story and highlighted by Paul in his letter to the Ephesians:

In love he predestined us for adoption to sonship through Jesus Christ.[7]

God has adopted us as his children. The wording that is used here in Paul's original language means the full standing of an adopted male in the Roman culture of his day. God has fully embraced us, fully brought us in and taken us into his heart. As John says in one of his shorter letters, 'See what great love the Father has lavished on us, that we should be called children of God! And that is what we are!'[8]

It is because Jesus has stood alongside us, shed his blood for us, fought the battle for us that we can be adopted into his family, that we can be called children of God. The blood of the covenant, the new relationship between God and creation enables us to experience not just new life but new life within the family of God. That is who we are, and that is where we belong.

A Slippery Slope

On a recent trip to Arlington Court on the edge of Exmoor National Park, we took Leo to a woodland adventure area. It was lots of climbing and running; mud, rocks, streams – all the things he loves. There was a steep muddy slope, about 15-feet high, leading down to the stream. The means of getting down this slope was a large rope with knots evenly spaced along it so that you could grip on your way down. Leo and I had made it safely down another slope earlier in the walk but Bex had walked the higher route. She eventually came to a point of either going back or coming down. Here was the problem: the rope was on the opposite side of the slope to Bex.

Now here is where I may have watched too many SAS programmes on TV because, in my head, this was a quick climb up, run the rope across the width of the slope to her, climb down and wait at the bottom, basking in my triumph.

Here's what happened. I climbed to the top fine, took the rope and heroically crossed the slope and passed it to Bex. Part one: check! As I was about to come down, I slipped on the wet mud, not only sliding down to the bottom but knocking Bex off the top with me as we both slid down the wet mud towards the stream. Fortunately, I was able to stop and catch Bex between my legs before we both ended up in the stream. Meanwhile, Leo had run off and was hopping over rocks across the stream almost out of sight. Bex was covered in mud all up her back and I had ripped my trousers. Part two: certainly no basking.

Sometimes it works out far better in your head than it does in reality. Real life is often much messier and far more bruising. Sadly, family can be one of those places too.

We have an idea of family, what it looks like, what it should be in our minds. A place of safety where we can thrive and become the best version of ourselves. A place where we can give and receive love in an affirming and nurturing way that builds solid foundations to help us in the rest of our lives. This is what we hope for. But what happens when the ground we stand on is slippery and we find ourselves tumbling downwards to find ourselves, at the least, disappointed, but sometimes in a great deal of pain?

A sense of belonging doesn't just happen. It takes time and commitment within a family for those within it to have a sense that they belong. Equally, when you have not experienced that within a family dynamic then it can be a painful reality to own, and a hard one to begin to work through.

I say that it is hard to own because the allure of the image of what our family should be is so strong. The hopes that we hold on to, even when they are shattered time and time again, are too strong to simply write people off or step away. And, often, to admit that our families are not the places we hoped them to be makes us feel as though, in doing so, we are affirming that we don't fit. Do we feel that it is better to feel we belong to a dysfunctional family and put up with that often-toxic dysfunctionality than to admit we don't belong and to feel on the outside? Perhaps there is some truth in that. As we have already seen, the pull to be part of the pack is strong.

Growing up within a healthy family environment provides an anchor for us as we move through life. What happens when that anchor isn't there? Psychotherapist Jasmin Lee Cori says, 'We can feel disconnected, lost and ungrounded in the world.'[9]

Is that something you have experienced? Does it feel at times as though you are drifting around the sea of life because you don't have that anchor to secure you when the winds come?

It is important to be able to honestly reflect on your family experience. Here are some key questions that you might want to ask as part of that reflection.

Do I feel as though I belong?

This is perhaps the hardest question because it may mean that we need to let go of and grieve some of the hopes that we have of what our families should be and look at them as they really are. You might have been hanging on to the hope that your family will change; that one day they will finally get you or see you for who you are and start meeting the needs that have been left unmet for such a long time. If that's the hope that you have been hanging on to, then let me tell you that there are many others who feel that too. It is not a bad hope to have, and you may have been patient and given your family many opportunities to change over time. It is a totally natural hope to have because it is based on the belief that family should be a place of safety and nurture and emotional richness and depth.

But we need to ask ourselves the question: is that my reality? If I keep finding myself in this place time and time again – of feeling as though I don't belong or feeling that the anchor is cut away each time – am I really belonging?

What would belonging within my family situation look like?

Reflecting in an honest way does not mean there is no place for hope. Quite the opposite; it allows our hopes to be realistic once we realize the position we are coming from.

There are no perfect families. Many of us know this already. Some have found that out all too painfully. If you think you are in that rare thing of a perfect family, then perhaps you haven't been going deep enough. I don't say that to burst your bubble but to help us to realize that with families, as with much of life, 'perfectionism is a curse'![10]

It is one of the most important skills we will ever develop . . . to learn what we need and have the courage to ask for it. However, to avoid the dangers of perfectionism, we may need to have a subtle word change which begins first in our own minds. Instead of thinking 'my family *should* be a place where I belong', we need to make the shift to think, 'my family *could/can* be a place where I belong if it looked like . . .' It might not seem like a big shift but letting go of the 'should' is harder than we might think.

What needs to change in order for that to become my reality?

Having pictured in our minds how our families could be, or can be, places where we belong, we need to think about what changes are needed in order to make that reality a possibility.

It might be that you need to sit down and have a conversation with your family, or key members of it, to work some of these things through. This might be a gradual process for you, or it might be that it comes more easily. It is well worth having some support from outside your family as you process these feelings and to work through what these steps might look like for you.

There may be changes that you have to make to yourself or about the way that you engage within the family dynamic. In the same way that our families are not perfect, we are not perfect either. Even though you are responsible for the changes you can make within yourself, you are not responsible for whether, or how, your family changes.

Before you move from reflecting on those questions internally, or with trusted others, into the possibility of sharing this within your family, remember that you don't have to rush – and that you don't *have to* share. You *could/can* share what you have reflected on, but for now, it might be that the reflection itself has been helpful for you, creating a mind-set shift or shining a new light on things you need to ponder some more.

Blocking the Flow

There is one more part of the slippery slope I want to reflect on with you as we think about belonging within our families. Favouritism.

> This is the story of Jacob. The story continues with Joseph, seventeen years old at the time, helping out his brothers in herding the flocks. These were his half-brothers actually, the sons of his father's wives Bilhah and Zilpah. And Joseph brought his father bad reports on them. Israel loved Joseph more than any of his other sons because he was the child of his old age. And he made him an elaborately embroidered coat. When his brothers realized that their father loved him more than them, they grew to hate him – they wouldn't even speak to him.[11]

Right at the start of the founding story of the Jewish and Christian faiths is Jacob, who was called Israel. Sometimes we talk about 'family' in the Bible with rose-tinted spectacles, but we don't need to look very far to see that they too had challenges and flaws and some of them deep indeed.

For Jacob, it was favouritism and we see it here in black and white: 'Israel loved Joseph more than any of his other sons.'

There were eleven other sons that needed the love and attention of their father, and this passage certainly does not say that Jacob didn't love them. In fact, the wording of the text implies that he did, it's just that he loved Joseph *more*.

What we see next is the justification: 'because he was the child of his old age'.

Hebrew scholar Robert Alter reflects: 'This explanation is a little odd, both because the fact that Joseph is the son of the beloved Rachel is unmentioned and because it is Benjamin who is the real child of Jacob's old age.'[12]

As with so much favouritism, it is left unsatisfactorily explained and, as in this case, comes partly to excuse questionable behaviour, namely Joseph's tale-telling on his brothers.

What is the response to this favouritism among the other brothers? They hated him and cut him off. This favouritism had brought hatred and brokenness into the family that gives their very names to the tribes that went on to form the nation of Israel.

It would be all too easy to say that Jacob should have known better, but in this case, we would be right. We only have to read back to Genesis 25 and we see a similar story. The favouritism of Jacob causes him to steal the dying blessing of his father from his older brother Esau. This brings great division and brokenness to their family. Once again no satisfactory reason is given to justify that favouritism.

Not only hasn't Jacob learned from his own experiences with his brother, which should have caused him to think twice about repeating those mistakes with Joseph, but even after Joseph has been sold into slavery in Egypt, he repeats the same mistake again with Benjamin. When Judah is explaining their family situation to the chief steward of Egypt, who he is unaware is his brother Joseph, he tells him:

> We have a father who is old and a younger brother who was born to him in his old age. His brother is dead and he is the only son left from that mother. And his father loves him more than *anything*.[13]

What does this example of favouritism show us? That favouritism works in the opposite spirit to belonging. Belonging is about having the freedom to give and receive within a family environment that is loving and mutual. Favouritism creates a block to that flow of giving and receiving because we only have a finite amount of love to give. If that love is directed disproportionately towards one individual, then it blocks the flow to the others. Not only that, but it creates an *elite* where one or some are held above the others because *the elite* is almost always at the expense of the rest. We see that within the structure of society, within faith and within family life. We see it within the story of Jacob and Joseph.

The challenge for us is to create, maintain and nurture family environments where all are treasured, valued and invested in, even if differently. Then family can be a place where all can belong rather than being a clique or the elite. Sometimes this may require us to re-evaluate, listen to, adapt and respond to the changing needs within the group as people grow rather than just continue to accept the established status quo that perhaps benefits one individual over the well-being of the whole. If we truly want to be a family where everyone equally and authentically belongs, we have to be willing to keep learning new dance steps along the way, otherwise there is a danger the rhythm of belonging may get lost, and once-close family members may find themselves on the outside edge, harbouring hurts, looking for new places to belong. Keeping a pack together is hard work and requires wisdom and sacrifice. There is no place for favouritism in a family when you want all to equally belong.

Before we move on, maybe pause here for a moment and ask yourself, is your place of belonging affected by favouritism? How does that make you feel? Are you aware some members of the pack feel like an underdog? What could you do to address that within your family either for yourself or as an act of love towards another on their behalf?

Or perhaps you could ask yourself if you have favourites within your group? Are there certain people or family members you automatically prefer to spend time with or find yourself more willingly directing your care and time in a certain direction? Perhaps you feel guilty because you know you show favouritism but you don't want to address it because you like the way things are. It brings you joy. Or maybe you're the one who is favoured and you don't want to share because you've got it good and you know it! But at whose expense? Not belonging is a foundational wound that can stunt growth. As we have seen with Isaac, Jacob and Joseph, there can be a generational trend towards that bias that we have an opportunity to challenge going forward.

In that spirit of challenge, I encourage you to spend some time reflecting on these things before God and see how he moves your heart to perhaps rebalance things out of love for the other members and their well-being, not just your own.

Take the Baton and Run!

Our history cannot be changed. What has led us to this moment cannot be altered. However, we can choose how we take hold of that and what we do next.

In the opening chapter of his helpful book *The Thriving Family*, David Coleman tries to help us understand what makes families thrive. As part of that, he encourages us to explore the situations we have come from and the family life we have experienced. He guides us:

If we know that elements of how we were raised had a negative impact on us, we may be eager to avoid replicating them . . .[14]

However, looking back endlessly will rob us from being able to move forwards. There will come a time when we need to take the baton, however it has been handed to us, and turn and set off on our leg of the race. There will be new family and new opportunities to craft a culture of belonging. Each generation has the ability to receive what has been before, but then to turn and run their leg of the race in their own way hoping that they can pass that baton on to the next generation in a helpful and meaningful way. How do you want to run? How can you help shape a culture of belonging within your family?

You may not be able to change how your family culture of belonging has been passed to your generation, but what you can do is run your own race. You can help to shape a new culture that avoids the pitfalls and mistakes of the past. Take hold of this precious gift and run, my friends. Run and dance in your own way . . . but make sure you do so in a way that draws others in, moving with them, flowing freely and filled with grace – creating and nurturing your family as a place where all within it can belong, and where the family as a whole can thrive.

5

The Community of the Church

'The supreme act of worship is to strive for biblical oneness.'[1]

A couple of years ago, we went on holiday to the coast, and while we were there, we decided to go to the local church on the Sunday. Leo was probably two years old at the time. We had visited this town many times and had often walked past the church, so we thought we would give it a try. When we entered the church nobody really spoke to us, and we were ushered into a small backroom behind the stage. There were some old toys on the floor, and the service was booming out over a loud speaker. The person who showed us in left, and we sat there wondering what was going on. Were there other children coming to join us? Was *anyone* else coming to join us? After a while it became clear that nobody was. So we decided to do something we hadn't done before: break out of church. There was no way that I was going to do the walk of shame, from behind the stage, through the congregation and out the front door. So I found a fire escape through a small corridor at the back, and we managed to get it open and escape into an alleyway that ran adjacent to the church.

Fortunately, we were able to laugh about it over a coffee, but at the same time, there was disappointment that a church community had failed to welcome us, a young family, on that day and make us feel included in their Sunday worship. Church on this occasion had not met our expectations.

What are your expectations of church? Some people have many, others have few. Some people think the church should focus inwards and others think it should be focused outwards. But is there one expectation, whatever our preference, that seems to be universal? That expectation to connect, to be part of a community, to belong. In his book *The Gospel According to Starbucks*, Leonard Sweet says:

> What is it people want most? What is it we are all searching for most desperately? The answer is one word with a million meanings: connectedness.[2]

That is why our experience in that holiday church was so disappointing; it was a missed opportunity to connect, and connection lies at the heart of the community of faith.

In March 2020, churches all over the world shut their doors because of the Covid-19 pandemic. This became a time of both challenge and opportunity for the church. A time of challenge because so much of what we do has been focused around being inside buildings, and all of a sudden, that was stripped away. Some certainly found this to be a challenge, but it was exactly here where the opportunities also lay. We now had the opportunity to express what it means to be church without the walls, without the programmes.

As a church, we had to decide how we were going to express what it means to belong when we physically couldn't meet together any more. Baptists will talk, although not exclusively, about the importance of the gathered church. All of a sudden there was no tangible gatheredness, no longer were we simply sharing a common space. Now it was about connectedness. How do we connect with one another? As a church, I am pleased to say that we responded quickly and had some things in place from the beginning. Once we made a decision to stop physically meeting and to close the church building, we knew that we needed to find new ways of connecting. Technology is always helpful in these situations, but with a church stacked at the older end of the age spectrum, I was worried that this would be difficult for people. I have been both surprised and delighted by the way the church has embraced these new ways of staying connected. Whether it is the church WhatsApp group, with half the church connecting with each other through that; our weekly Zoom catch-up; daily thoughts for the day on the church's YouTube channel or just calling people each day to talk to them; we are finding new ways to belong to each other and to be connected as a church.

Many in the church have spoken about a new closeness that we are experiencing because of this. Why? Because deep down within us there is that need to belong, that desire to connect with others, especially when the possibility of doing that face to face has been taken away. We could have all simply bunkered down for the Covid-19 winter in some sort of relational hibernation. Instead we chose – were driven to reach out – to find new ways to belong together as church (and across churches) because there is a drive deep within us to do so that cannot be suppressed. Because unity is not simply a hoped-for destination but it is the reality of who we are. It cannot be locked down. Our buildings may be shut but the church is alive!

However, it is not something we have always modelled well as the church.

A History of Broken Connection

It is not just a realistic expectation for the church to be a place of connectedness but it is also the goal. Connection with God, connection with each other and connection with the world. When our churches fail to be places of genuine connection, then we are losing something of what church is really meant to be.

I remember one of the most difficult modules during my time training at Spurgeon's Bible College was 'Church History'. It wasn't so much the difficulty of the work as it was being confronted time and time again with division within the life of the church.

Whether it was the split between the church in the East and West in 1054 or the reformation in the sixteenth century or many other splits in-between, the church has not had a great track record modelling to the world a way to hold difference.

Then you had the argument that existed within the church about what happened at communion. Does the bread mysteriously become the physical body and blood of Jesus or does it simply represent and take on that significance in that meal? How it must pain the heart of God that this meal, given as a principle means and sign of the unity of the church, has become the focal point for its disunity.

The number of martyrs killed – not by those of different faiths or none but by those who equally profess to follow Jesus as Lord – is staggering.

What has this got to do with belonging?

In John 13, Jesus says to his disciples:

> A new command I give you: love one another. As I have loved you, so you must love one another. By this everyone will know that you are my disciples, if you love one another.[3]

It is not our doctrinal adherence or our ethical purity or our evangelistic zeal which will demonstrate our belonging to Christ. It is our love; our love for one another.

So when the church has historically failed to hear the voice of the other, then it has failed to live its identity as the body of Christ.

In an interview on 27 September 1966, Martin Luther King said that 'a riot is the language of the unheard'. When we fail to hear each other, to listen in love and seek to understand the other's position, then what comes from that is often a riot. This was not just true of the civil rights struggle in the United States but it has been true of the church of Jesus Christ for almost two thousand years. When we can hold difference well, we not only love one another but we create a space for each other to be able to give and receive freely. If we fail to listen and the voices of those who differ are silenced or blocked out, then that place of belonging becomes a place of exclusion even within the walls of a church building.

The church operates at its best when living as a radical and counter-cultural community of love, creating space for connectedness with God, one another and the world; a place of belonging where each member finds their voice.

Belong to One Another

Have you ever looked around in church and wondered, 'Outside of this setting, when would I ever spend time with these people?' Not because you don't like them, hopefully, but because church draws in different types of people from different settings and backgrounds with different interests and passions. It is a beautiful community of embraced difference which seeks to create a space for all.

One of the challenges that we have in today's church culture is that we tend to talk about belonging to *a* church rather than *the* church. We tend to express connection to an institution rather than a community of people. Within my own Baptist community that has all too often been the case. That those current 'members' of the church are the current custodians of that role, passed on to them from those who came before, to keep the cogs of the great machine turning. Rather, we are not custodians but companions on a journey, pilgrims walking each other home. We belong not to an institution but to one another. After all, isn't that what the apostle Paul was talking to the church in Rome about?

> For by the grace given me I say to every one of you: do not think of yourself more highly than you ought, but rather think of yourself with sober judgment, in accordance with the faith God has distributed to each of you. For just as each of us has one body with many members, and these members do not all have the same function, so in Christ we, though many, form one body, and each member belongs to all the others. We have different gifts, according to the grace given to each of us. If your gift is prophesying, then prophesy in accordance with your faith; if it is serving, then serve; if it is teaching, then teach; if it is to encourage, then give encouragement; if it is giving, then give generously; if it is to lead, do it diligently; if it is to show mercy, do it cheerfully. Love must be sincere. Hate what is evil; cling to what is good. Be devoted to one another in love. Honour one another above yourselves.[4]

There is a lot of wisdom here to unpack when it comes to creating a space for belonging within the life of the church.

The first part of this passage deals with humility. Now the common problem with humility is that we tend to think that it means we need to think less of ourselves. When we hear verses like those in Philippians chapter 2 that view tends to be reinforced:

> Rather, in humility value others above yourselves, not looking to your own interests but each of you to the interests of the others.[5]

What does it mean to value others above yourself? *The Message* puts it like this:

> Forget yourself long enough to lend a helping hand.

In his book *A Purpose Driven Life*, Rick Warren summarized the words of C.S. Lewis in *Mere Christianity*: 'Humility is not thinking less of yourself, but thinking about yourself less.'[6]

In order to create space in church for people to belong, we need to have a sense of individual and corporate humility. Places where we think less of our own preferences and needs and more about the needs of the other. That sounds good, other than we sometimes worry that our own needs will be ignored. The beauty of this culture is that, in ensuring all are focusing on the needs of the other, everyone's needs should be met. Your needs will be met by the others in the community. The hard thing to do is to let go of the absolute control of your care and allow others to share in it, which involves trust. What is even harder is to let others share in it when you have been hurt, which does happen even within church communities.

When we are humble in this way, we open up the channels of giving and receiving within our lives and our life together, which is at the heart of what it means to belong. It allows us to model a vulnerability, a mutuality, a common movement towards one another; a beautiful dance in which I am constantly

met in my meeting of you, and you in me. A place of acceptance and holding which is both light and free as well as outra-
geously dynamic.

We also need to be humble corporately. We need to be open
to those outside of our communities whether that is other
churches we work in partnership with, the community as a
whole or individuals outside of the community. As Jean Vanier,
founder of the L'Arche community said, 'Communities are
truly communities when they are open to others.'[7]

Are our churches communities which are open to others? If the
measure of our humility is our ability to focus on the needs of
others, then are our churches focused on the needs of those on the
outside? Are our programmes, cultures, preferences and energy directed towards the stranger in the community or to ourselves? Are
we cultivating a place, not only for us to belong, but for others?

This coming weekend we have a church away morning. It's a
great opportunity to get together, share and grow in friendship
and explore what it means to be church in Bath today. This
time we are focusing on three questions:

1. Who are we – what makes us unique?
2. Why are we here – who are we serving?
3. How then should we live?

Focusing on ourselves and others and tying that together in a
life lived out in our actions not just our beliefs.

The next part of our passage from Romans 12 talks to us
about the different roles that people play within the life of the
church. Let's just recap what Paul said:

> For just as each of us has one body with many members, and
> these members do not all have the same function, so in Christ
> we, though many, form one body . . .

This section of Paul's letter to the Romans is a much shorter version of the thought that he writes to the church in Corinth about:

Just as a body, though one, has many parts, but all its many parts form one body, so it is with Christ. For we were all baptized by one Spirit so as to form one body – whether Jews or Gentiles, slave or free – and we were all given the one Spirit to drink. And so the body is not made up of one part but of many. Now if the foot should say, 'Because I am not a hand, I do not belong to the body,' it would not for that reason stop being part of the body. And if the ear should say, 'Because I am not an eye, I do not belong to the body,' it would not for that reason stop being part of the body. If the whole body were an eye, where would the sense of hearing be? If the whole body were an ear, where would the sense of smell be? But in fact God has placed the parts in the body, every one of them, just as he wanted them to be. If they were all one part, where would the body be? As it is, there are many parts, but one body. The eye cannot say to the hand, 'I don't need you!' And the head cannot say to the feet, 'I don't need you!' On the contrary, those parts of the body that seem to be weaker are indispensable, and the parts that we think are less honourable we treat with special honour. And the parts that are unpresentable are treated with special modesty, while our presentable parts need no special treatment. But God has put the body together, giving greater honour to the parts that lacked it, so that there should be no division in the body, but that its parts should have equal concern for each other. If one part suffers, every part suffers with it; if one part is honoured, every part rejoices with it. Now you are the body of Christ, and each one of you is a part of it. And God has placed in the church first of all apostles, second prophets, third teachers, then miracles, then gifts of healing, of helping,

of guidance, and of different kinds of tongues. Are all apostles?
Are all prophets? Are all teachers? Do all work miracles? Do all
have gifts of healing? Do all speak in tongues? Do all interpret?
Now eagerly desire the greater gifts.[8]

There are two specific things I want to highlight from this passage, which are also expressed in our Romans passage. Firstly,
that church is a place where everyone has a part to play. I am
stressing this all the time at our church. Not because I want
people to do more, although there is always a lot to do, but
because I want them to know that what they do matters. I want
them to feel a sense of investment in who we are as a church.
I want them to experience a sense of knowing that what they
contribute makes a difference. That without so many who give
their time, their energy and their gifts, the church as we express
it here would not be able to function. That's what Paul is saying
towards the end of the passage in 1 Corinthians: 'Now you are
the body of Christ, and *each one of you* is a part of it.' Each one
of you! Not just those who can play the guitar and sing. Not
just those who can speak well from the front. Not just those
who seem to lead someone to Jesus every time they are in the
checkout queue in Sainsbury's. Each one of you. That you are
integral to the life of the community and without you the community would be less than what it is. That we foster a sense of
belonging when we give space for each person to have a place
and a role. When people feel as though they can contribute
to the life of the community, then their sense of belonging is
enhanced.

Secondly, each person and role within the church will look
different. So often we seem to think that unity means uniformity. How utterly boring an expression of togetherness that would
be in light of a God of wondrous creativity. Not only do we all

have a place within the life of the church but we are all different. The way we express our faith, live it out, and serve will be different. Talking about the apostle Paul in his book *Discovering Your Place in the Body of Christ*, Selwyn Hughes says:

> His desire for every newly formed church was that they might develop their ministries in harmony with God's personal plan for their lives.[9]

Your role within the life of the church will be 'you-shaped'. Not what others say you are – although sometimes the support of others can be helpful in discerning how we might find our place – but the you that God says you are according to his plan for your life.

It might be that you are reading this and wondering what your gift is, what your role might be. It might be helpful to talk to those who know you well, family and friends, perhaps people in your small group, your pastor. Always make sure, though, that you take what they say and weigh it yourself and ask, 'Does this fit with who I believe God has created me to be?'

Before we move on to the last part of this passage, I want to leave you with an image to reflect on.

In their beautiful book *What is My Song?*,[10] Matt, Sheila and Dennis Linn give us the image of an African tribe. Within this tribe each person has a song which is theirs. It holds within it the truth of who a person is, the hopes of which are expressed by their parents before they are born. Each child is taught to sing their song. When they forget who they are, then the village will gather around them and sing that song to them to remind them. When they reach key milestones in life, this song is sung. When they die, the villagers gather around and sing this song for the last time.

What a beautiful image – not just of the individuality of each of us having a song but in the community that knows us and helps us to grow into who we are. The book is written for children because it is important that from a young age we are able to explore, along with those around us, what our song is.

In their book *Healing the Purpose of Your Life*,[11] aimed at adults, Matt, Sheila and Dennis write: 'Just as God sent John the Baptist ahead with sealed orders to prepare the way for Jesus, what if God sends people along with every one of us?'[12]

What is your song? What is it that only you can uniquely express? Are you part of a church community that can hear, learn and sing that song back to you? That's part of what it means to belong.

The last point I want to focus on within this passage from Romans 12 is a short phrase which sometimes gets lost but which contains some of the most profound words about what it means to belong to a church that I have ever read. We find them at the end of verse five: 'each member belongs to all the others'.

Those seven words are some of the most challenging to our consumer church culture that you will find in the Bible. That I am not just called to belong to a church but I am called to belong to the people who make it up. That they are *my people* and I am *theirs*. That, as Jean Vanier says, 'Whether we are near each other or far away, my brothers and sisters remain written within me. I carry them, and they, me.'[13]

What does that look like in reality? I have a particular person in mind in my church. I'll call him Adam. Adam and I are from different generations; we have had different upbringings, different social and political leanings. We have very different ideas of what church is and how that should be expressed. We are very different people.

What does it mean for me to belong to him and for him to belong to me? Those are terms that we would probably struggle to embrace for each other. At times, we actively shy away from them. But there is the reality. There it is in black and white. *Each* member belongs to the others. Not just those we warm to or connect with or like – but *each* one.

Much like the prayer of Jesus in John 17, that his disciples may be one just as he and the Father are one, there is great mystery here. The challenge brings with it a great opportunity. Even though at times it is hard to visualize what this would look like with Adam, the opportunity is to work towards it. Will I work towards opening a space in my heart for Adam to belong? Will I be prepared to take up a space in his heart? That begins, as it so often does, with prayer. Will I pray for Adam, for God's deep and rich blessing to saturate his life? Will I pray that God prospers him and helps him to thrive? Will I pray that God helps me to open up that space in my heart? That, before I can belong to Adam, I need to accept him. Accept him as he is and accept that he is mine, not possessively, but that God has given him to me to love, nurture and support. After all, later in Romans, Paul encourages us to do just that: 'Accept one another, then, just as Christ accepted you, in order to bring praise to God.'[14]

Accepting one another, as God has accepted us, is one of the first and most important steps to belonging within church and creating a culture within church where people can belong. After all, as Jürgen Moltmann reminds us: 'Human beings need acceptance just as the birds need air and the fish water. Acceptance is the atmosphere of humanity.'[15]

Let's open our hearts to one another and, in doing so, create in us and find in others a home, a place of blessing and belonging.

Belong, Believe, Behave

In the first church I served in as a minister, we spent a year looking at 'Kingdom Living'. We structured this year with the words 'Belong, Believe, Behave'.

In the section called 'belong' we looked at issues such as communion, baptism, membership, leadership, worship and service.

The section looking at 'believe' covered themes including eternity, God as creator, God as Father, Holiness, Prayer, Sin and the Trinity.

The section entitled 'behave' looked at being a devoted follower, care for the planet, family life, forgiveness, God in the darkness, judging others and marriage.

There are some themes on that list that I would take away and others that I would add in, over a decade in ministry later.

What I want to focus on for a moment is the three words we based the series around: 'belong, believe, behave'.

We chose the order of the words carefully. As a team we had certainly come across churches that would have chosen to order them differently: believe, behave, belong. They would say that the first and most important part of that process is that you believe certain things about God, then that you live in a way that reflects that belief and that, once these two primary parts of the process are in place, you can belong to the community.

We were in no doubt that all three of these words were important, but we wanted to emphasize and model the order differently.

Belong – it is very often belonging that happens first. People are drawn into a community of faith, and through the love, welcome and acceptance of those in that community, they see something of God which draws them closer to him. As Jesus himself said to his followers:

By this everyone will know that you are my disciples, if you have love for one another.[16]

It is that experience of love flowing out and drawing in that reflects something deep about the love of God, which creates that space to belong from which all else flows.

There is an interesting account in the gospels of Jesus meeting a rich young man:

As he was setting out on a journey, a man ran up and knelt before him, and asked him, 'Good Teacher, what must I do to inherit eternal life?' Jesus said to him, 'Why do you call me good? No one is good but God alone. You know the commandments: "You shall not murder; You shall not commit adultery; You shall not steal; You shall not bear false witness; You shall not defraud; Honour your father and mother."' He said to him, 'Teacher, I have kept all these since my youth.' Jesus, looking at him, loved him and said, 'You lack one thing; go, sell what you own, and give the money to the poor, and you will have treasure in heaven; then come, follow me.' When he heard this, he was shocked and went away grieving, for he had many possessions.[17]

In this passage we have these three elements: belong, believe and behave. The phrase that strikes me comes in the first part of verse 21: 'Jesus, looking at him, loved him . . .'

We see that throughout the gospels. Jesus accepting and welcoming. Here it is a socially accepted person, but we also see Jesus welcome and accept those who society would easily reject:

The Samaritan woman in John 4.
Those suffering from leprosy in Luke 17.
The woman caught in adultery in John 8.

These are just a few of many whom society rejected but whom Jesus welcomes. They do not have to have taken a membership class or signed a statement of faith. But they are accepted as who they are. They are seen and, in that seeing, they were welcomed.

Think about the disciples who Jesus called. Many of them were from 'lower' professions in their day. They were not the academic or spiritual elite, but Jesus calls them anyway. He calls them because he is creating a culture, a kingdom which does not belong to the powerful and the privileged, the elite and the educated. It belongs to those who are willing to follow, who are willing to leave their lives behind in order to gain a fuller, richer and deeper life. It is this life that many are seeking and yet it is available right now, in this very moment. People do not come to church seeking religion – at least I hope not. And if they do, then I hope they are disappointed. It is this life, this full, rich and deep life that Jesus offers, expressed (although sometimes poorly) through his church that people come seeking. It is here, within this life, that they want to belong.

Believe – When you have had this experience of Jesus as the one who welcomes, you then have a place of safety to explore who this Jesus really is. The response of belief came after acceptance and belonging. Having received that, people want to know about the God who offers it and, in this case, offers it through his people.

Belief is far more than signing up to a set of doctrines or rules. It is far deeper than simply adherence to a moral code. So often we have cheapened it by expressing it in this way.

Belief is a living response to a living encounter with a living God. When Jesus spoke to his disciples before his passion, he reassured them by saying, 'Do not let your hearts be troubled. Believe in God, believe also in me.'[18]

The word 'believe' here is from the Greek πιστεύετε. This is the most favoured translation. However, this word can also be translated as 'trust'. Our response to the welcome of God and the experience of belonging is to put our trust in this God. The word 'trust' is much more relational and reflects the ongoing nature of the journey of faith that we are all on.

When it is seen and experienced in this way, then it can lead to transformation. That transformation can change the way we see everything, and can change every aspect of our lives.

Behave – this word is far from ideal, and there are times when I think it was simply chosen to keep the alliteration of 'B'. What it seeks to express is less 'good behaviour' and more 'life response'. I have experienced what it means to be accepted and to belong; I have believed and chosen to place my trust in the God who has accepted and welcomes me; and now that I am experiencing that transformation, I want that to flow across every area of my life, my actions and behaviours.

This transformation does not come as a result of our own effort but as a result of the Spirit of God making a home in our lives. What happens then is that our 'behaviour' starts to bear the delicious fruit of that transformed life.

> The fruit of the Spirit is love, joy, peace, forbearance, kindness, goodness, faithfulness, gentleness and self-control.[19]

Are our churches places of belonging? Are they places of encounter, both with God and with his people? There is a phrase that I remember from when our son was a toddler: parallel play. Basically, it is when two or more children are playing in the same room but really they are doing their own thing. They might be playing in the same space, but they are not playing together – rather, they are playing in parallel. Sometimes church can be a bit like that. We are sharing the same space, but we aren't really part of a shared experience. Each comes and sings the songs, prays the prayers, hears the word and takes the sacrament, but in parallel rather than together.

Do we leave feeling that we have connected? With God and with each other?

Does our insistence that a person's behaviour has to be right before they can belong really show the love and acceptance of God? Does it reflect his welcome? Do people look at the way we love each other in church and see something of God?

These are all important questions and ones that we, as churches, must continue to wrestle with if we are to be life-giving communities that show the transforming welcome of God, and who create spaces where all can belong.

I think about my own church context. If a person wants to become a church member then there is a process that they have to go through. I'm not sure that the process doesn't cause more harm than good. I sometimes describe it provocatively like this: 'If you want to become a member then the church will ask two members to come and interview you. They will then give a report to a meeting that you are not allowed to go to. Those who are at the meeting will then vote on whether they feel that you should be a member of the church.' And we wonder why membership in churches is down!

In reality, it is nowhere near as bad as it sounds. The 'interview' is an informal chat, usually over coffee, to hear something of a person's story so that it can be faithfully shared with the meeting. When it is shared, it is often done so in an excited and loving way, and in over a decade of ministry, I have never experienced a person not wholeheartedly be accepted into membership.

I am left wondering, though, what would happen if a person who wasn't 'like us' asked to come into membership? Someone who didn't fit the mould? Would the process feel as harmless as we think it is? You see one of the problems with the model is that it often portrays an 'in or out' model of belonging. You really belong if you are a member. It essentially works on contracts and commitments. As Joseph Myers rightly reflects, though, 'people crave connections, not contracts'.[20]

When that connection happens outside of the 'contract' it is a beautiful thing. I remember in my previous church, during an anniversary service we asked members to stand up as an act of commitment. One lady stood up who was not formally a church member and afterwards said to me that she wasn't sure if she should be standing or not, but she did because she felt that she belonged!

When we get it right, when we reflect something of that precious belonging and welcome of Jesus, then it transcends all barriers and structures, drawing us closer to God and to each other. Then we are a community. Then we are church. Then we have a place to belong.

6

Belonging to God

'We're all united to God, but only some of us know it. Most of us deny and doubt it.'[1]

Where do you begin when seeking to write a chapter on what it means to belong to God? Like pouring a pint of water into a half-pint glass, there will always be more than we could possibly ever hold. Or it is like standing out in a wide-open space, under a big sky and taking in a deep breath. Your lungs are full, you cannot fit anything more into them, but there is more air to be breathed in; so much more. No matter how many breaths you take, or how deeply you breathe, there will always be more. Yet God, so graciously, so humbly stoops down to be described in words that he, and we, know are wholly inadequate.

I can say that I love my wife and son and, in the same breath, say that I love pizza. I can say that I love Tottenham Hotspur Football Club and, in the same breath, say I love God. It's the same word but the concept is totally different. It gets even more difficult when I turn my attention to God's love. When I use the word 'love' of God, I am having to deal with a limited concept trying to describe something limitless. You see, what I understand love to be is shaped by the love I have experienced. I have experienced love given beautifully and freely, and I have experienced love given sparingly and begrudgingly. All of this is packaged up within the term love. God, however, will not be wrapped up so neatly. The love that is at the centre of who God is, eternally and unchangingly, burns through any attempts to limit it or contain it. Yet, at the same time, the God whose love cannot be tamed stoops down to allow me to put my broken understanding onto him. He wears it lightly though, not defined by it but wearing it constantly as a challenge to how I see things and an invitation to come and experience something more. That God says, 'Yes, I love you, at least as much as you understand love to be, but at the most, more than you could possibly ever contain.'

In that sense, what I am doing in this chapter is much like a child at the seaside. I am running down to the water's edge of the great ocean, scooping up a bucket of water and running back with it to show you. I wonder at this bucket of water with childlike wonder: this bucket contains the ocean but, at the same time, it does not contain the ocean. As I wonder at the contents of this bucket, just behind me is the great and vast ocean that stretches beyond that which I can see, beyond the capacity of my vision, beyond the limits of my imagination and beyond that which my tiny hands can measure.

Even though my language might not be enough, my friend Dr Nigel Wright reminds us:

> It may be inadequate but it is not inaccurate. It is limited in speaking of the greatest of all mysteries but it is not misleading.[2]

All of this is a challenge when we come to look at a chapter like this. So the chapter comes with a warning and an invitation. The warning is that anything I can say about this is woefully short of what it means to really belong to God. The invitation comes in that, when what we say about God is accurate, he is constantly inviting us, you and me, to come and discover more of who he really is and more of who we are at the same time. Hear the warning, and accept the invitation as we journey on.

It's Who You Are

When we talk about *belonging* to God it can sound a little possessive. For God, though, belonging is less about what he has, as it is about who he is. He is the God of belonging, the God of relationship, the God who freely gives and freely receives, not just to the cosmos but within who God eternally is.

We often use the word Trinity to describe the separateness of God as Father, Son and Holy Spirit.[3] Again, we are trying to pour a pint of water into a half-pint glass. God can be distinct while at the same time being uncompromisingly united.

We can see this as we look throughout the Bible.

The Jewish people have a very special prayer called the 'Shema'. It is the climax point of the liturgy on the day of atonement and is, traditionally, the prayer prayed before death. It is written on a small scroll and placed in a Mezuzah on the doorpost of the house. It was a prayer that Jesus knew, and a prayer Jesus would have prayed almost every day. You can find it in Deuteronomy:

Hear, O Israel: the Lord our God, the Lord is one.[4]

Within Judaism, this was a numerical expression. There is *one* God. So the idea central to Christianity that God is Father, Son and Holy Spirit seems to be a betrayal of one of their most precious and central beliefs. However, 'one' in this prayer is not a number, it is a relationship. It is a unity. As Tim Chester puts it:

> God always speaks with one voice. Father, Son and Spirit speak with one voice because they are one . . . Yahweh has a unity of will and a constancy of character.[5]

Or as Wright puts it:

> The unity of God is a three-dimensional unity.[6]

So what is this constancy of character that Chester speaks about? Love. As John so beautifully puts it: 'God is love.'[7]

God exists in perfect loving relationship as Father, Son and Spirit, in beautiful and dynamic oneness. It is in the giving and receiving of this love between them that we see who God is for all eternity. God's oneness is not static, it is dynamic. It is not stone, it is flow. God is community. God is belonging.

This is a challenge to us because we like to think of things as concrete, as black and white. We like rules, we like laws. We like it when God plays by our rules, when he is in a box we can carry around with us, when he is in a temple we have built for him or when he meets with us in the hour-long window each week we have set aside for him.

Here's the thing that will challenge our theology. God does not play by our rules, he doesn't fit into our boxes, he is not confined by our temples and he isn't limited by our schedule.

God IS. The name he gave to Moses at the burning bush: I Am. I am who I was; I will be who I am. For God this self-revelation is not restrictive, but it is utter freedom to be who God eternally and unchangingly is.

What does this have to do with the Trinity? When we accept that God is far more dynamic and relational than we can possibly understand or imagine, it frees us up to experience the very thing that makes God so dynamic and unified in the first place: his love.

As we look at what it means to belong to God, it is also helpful for us to look at the different persons of the Trinity.

The Father

My baptismal verse was the first part of 1 John 3:

> See what great love the Father has lavished on us, that we should be called children of God! And that is what we are![8]

Growing up, I found it hard to relate to God as Father. It is since I have become a father myself that my journey to belonging to God as Father has deepened. I had no issue with God as Father, and I have had two wonderful dads who have shown me something of who God is as a father. It's just, when Leo was born, I experienced that at a deeper level.

Leo has just turned four and is so full of life. This morning I sat in the play room with him while he did a collage of a T-Rex with feathers. He wanted me to sit with him while he did it. He always wants us to watch what he is doing, to give him affirmation and support and to show an interest in him. We don't always get it right as parents, but we try every day to learn from the times we get it wrong to be better parents in the future.

I want to be a good father to my son. I want to support him, to nurture him, to cuddle and kiss him. I want him to know, beyond doubt, even when it's tough, that I love him. I would give up my life for him in a moment. I want him to have the fullness of every good thing about me and I want to protect him from the parts of me which fall short. Jesus said:

> Which of you, if your son asks for bread, will give him a stone? Or if he asks for a fish, will give him a snake? If you, then, though you are evil, know how to give good gifts to your children, how much more will your Father in heaven give good gifts to those who ask him![9]

If I, who am far from perfect as a father, want those things for my child, how much more does God want and provide what is good for us as his children. Love, life, freedom, grace, hope, peace . . . the list goes on with unending favour; not because of how good I am as a child but because of how good he is as a Father.

There is an intimacy in that parent-child relationship which we miss if we fail to connect with God as Father. We see that language in the way Jesus talks about his Father in Mark's gospel. When Jesus is praying in the garden of Gethsemane, he prays:

> '*Abba*, Father,' he said, 'everything is possible for you. Take this cup from me. Yet not what I will, but what you will.'[10]

The word '*abba*' that Jesus uses here is an Aramaic word of affection from a child to a father. It is not formal but intimate. It's the word that Leo calls me . . . Daddy.

That is the depth of intimacy that Jesus has with the Father, the depth of intimacy the Father has with his children.

We see this beautiful language of belonging right back in the prophet Isaiah:

> But now thus says the LORD, he who created you, O Jacob, he who formed you, O Israel: Do not fear, for I have redeemed you; I have called you by name, you are mine.[11]

Child, you belong to me, you are mine!

The Son

Paul says to the church in Ephesus:

> Now you belong to Christ Jesus. At one time you were far away from God. Now you have been brought close to Him.[12]

How do we belong to Jesus? The constant call of Jesus to women and men throughout the gospels was clear but far from simple: 'Follow me.' If we want to belong to Jesus, then it is more than an academic acceptance of the truth of the Christian faith. It is more than a religious observance of certain rights and rituals. It is following him. It is becoming like him. That is the nature of discipleship . . . becoming like the one you follow, doing what the rabbi does. That's what we read in Romans 8:

> For those God foreknew he also predestined to be conformed to the image of his Son, that he might be the firstborn among many brothers and sisters.[13]

For those who want to come to Jesus, the journey and the destination is that we become more like Jesus. The destination is not a somewhere but a *someone*. Our belonging is not to an ideal or to a religion but it is to the person of Jesus.

If we want to truly follow Jesus today, then there needs to be an openness and transformation. An openness to offer God all that we are, have been and hope to be so that transformation can occur. This transformation is not uniformity! It is not that God wants a family of clones in the same way that unity in God as Father, Son and Holy Spirit does not mean uniformity. Diversity is celebrated in the heart of God and it is celebrated in the mission and redemption of God too. God's plan and purpose for you is not that you become Christ but that *you* become *like* Christ, and then, in that transformation, you become more fully you as well.

In Jesus we see the blueprint for humanity, a humanity set free from all its imperfections to reflect clearly the image of God. In Jesus we find our true humanity. To belong to Jesus, to follow Jesus, to become like Jesus is to belong more fully to our human family and to belong to God himself.

The Spirit

Unfortunately, God the Holy Spirit has probably been the most misunderstood and misrepresented member of the Trinity over the years. R.T. Kendall, reflecting on the Holy Spirit coming down from heaven like a dove at Jesus' baptism, challenges us that sometimes we can settle for a pigeon when what we really need is the dove: 'It seems to me that many claims to be the presence of the Dove amongst us are but pigeon religion.'[14]

There are lots of possible reasons for this, and I don't think we need to spend time reflecting on those now. What it is important to reflect upon is what we know we can say about the Holy Spirit.

First, we can say that Jesus was full of the Holy Spirit. After Jesus had been baptized in Luke 3, Luke 4 opens with these words:

> Jesus, full of the Holy Spirit, left the Jordan and was led by the Spirit into the wilderness . . .[15]

This was not just a case of a special anointing, but as R.T. Kendall reflects, 'The Holy Spirit was at home with Jesus. They were mutually adjusted to each other.'[16]

Jesus is showing us, within this new humanity, a new relationship of belonging to God through the Holy Spirit. God was not just making his home with us but making his home *in* us. That the God of creation, the God of the vastness of all that is, the untameable and uncontainable, is choosing to come and live in you and me. That this belonging enters a new and intimate place of shared space. That the God who is perfect relationship within himself, perfect belonging and freedom, is pitching his tent, is moving in, not just to my neighbourhood but to my very heart! How can we find language for that?

The Spirit living within us, God within us, will be the means through which all we see of the Father and the Son come to find their settled place within us. As Paul says to the church in Galatia:

> Because you are children, God has sent the Spirit of his Son into our hearts, crying, 'Abba! Father!' So you are no longer a slave but a child, and if a child then also an heir, through God.[17]

We have already seen that we are God's children, and because (as John says) that is what we are, God has given us a level of intimacy with him, a way of belonging to him. This relationship is all about belonging. We are not slaves to religion or some moral taskmaster in the clouds but we are children, loved, beloved and treasured. Through our belonging to him, we inherit all that he freely offers to us.

May They Be in Us

There are some times when you come across parts of the Bible that are so full of mind-blowing beauty that a lifetime of reflection would never be enough to fully get your head around it. One of those passages is a prayer prayed by Jesus himself in John 17. Having prayed for himself and for his disciples, Jesus continues his prayer to pray for those who come to faith through the message of the gospel. That's you and me. Let this sink in for a moment. We don't simply pray to Jesus but Jesus prays for us. Here is that prayer:

> My prayer is not for them [the disciples] alone. I pray also for those who will believe in me through their message, that all of them may be one, Father, just as you are in me and I am in you. May they also be in us so that the world may believe that you have sent me. I have given them the glory that you gave me, that they may be one as we are one – I in them and you in me – so that they may be brought to complete unity. Then the world will know that you sent me and have loved them even as you have loved me. Father, I want those you have given me to be with me where I am, and to see my glory, the glory you have given me because you loved me before the creation of the world. Righteous Father, though the world does not know you, I know you, and they know that you have sent me. I have made

you known to them, and will continue to make you known in order that the love you have for me may be in them and that I myself may be in them.[18]

What incredible words. Where do we begin with such a prayer? Again, we see that same intimate language we have already explored. There are several key elements to his prayer that are worth exploring more.

Unity with each other

That all of them may be one.[19]

We are called to be united with each other. We see that so many times throughout the Bible:

How good and pleasant it is when God's people live together in unity! It is like precious oil poured on the head, running down on the beard, running down on Aaron's beard, down on the collar of his robe. It is as if the dew of Hermon were falling on Mount Zion. For there the LORD bestows his blessing, even life forevermore.[20]

There is blessing in unity. And unity is Jesus' prayer for us as his followers. How we hear that prayer in the context of denominations and church splits is sometimes challenging. Where I agree with fellow disciples on the road of faith or not, it doesn't matter, we are both on the road together. Some would want to throw in at this point that there has to be some standard of orthodoxy, and I'm not disputing that there does. That has been the same conversation the church has been having for the past two thousand years, and we still struggle with unity. No matter what my differences with other Christians or disagreements about what we believe, I cannot get away from this prayer of Jesus. His prayer, for you and me, is that we shall be one.

What if we were to frame our conversations about doctrine and dogma around this prayer? Not statements of faith, or creeds, but this prayer. What if our statements of faith and creeds were funnelled through the words of this prayer? What a change that would make.

Again, that unity is not meant to be uniformity because this prayer and longing for our unity is that it be based on the unity within God himself as Father, Son and Holy Spirit.

God's diversity within himself is a model for our diversity in belonging to each other.

That unity can really only exist, not in common purpose or common activity, but in a common dwelling within God himself:

> Jesus here envisages a profound spiritual intimacy that changes human life. It is unity encompassing the Father with the Son, the disciples with them both, and the disciples in union with one another.[21]

Unity with God

> Just as you are in me and I am in you. May they also be in us . . .[22]

When we come to this part of the prayer, this is where our language falls short again. Here I know how woefully small my bucket is! Mystery, far from being the absence of meaning, is the presence of so much meaning that we cannot possibly contain it.

So my hope here is to simply offer you two images through which I hope you can take a certain truth away.

The first image is of an icon that has come to mean a lot to me in recent years. I did not grow up with any understanding of what an icon was, nor did we have any at home or in church. I have two in my office. The one I am referring to is sometimes called 'Abraham's visitors'[23] but is more often called 'Icon of the Trinity'. It was painted by Russian artist Andrei Rublev in the early fifteenth century and depicts the three figures who visit Abraham in Genesis 18. Traditionally, they have been interpreted within the icon to be Father, Son and Holy Spirit – the Trinity. They are sitting at a table together, sharing food, with a house in the background.

The figures sitting at the table create the focus of the icon, with one sitting on the left of the table as we look at it, one behind the table and one on the right. It leaves the fourth side of the table, the one directly in front of the observer, open.

It is this openness that creates the deep sense of meaning for me when I look at this icon. There is a space opening up, right in front of me, at this table of fellowship, of joyous relationship. There is an invitation here; I am drawn into the meal that is being shared by Father, Son and Holy Spirit. As Richard Rohr puts it, 'Even this Three-Fullness does not like to eat alone.'[24]

Even the shape that the Three make outlines a cup, as if the very relationship between them, the bonds between them, are a cup of blessing that both pours out and draws in.

Rohr goes on to speak of this in very scientific terms as centrifugal (moving outwards) and centripetal (moving inwards) love.[25] Love that is always flowing outward from the eternal relationship of who God is in love as Father, Son and Holy Spirit; but also drawn in to relationship with God's self all that God has made. What a deep mystery! What a stunning invitation!

Not only does the love of God flow out to you and me, that we receive it, but it also draws us in so that we might experience and give love to God too. Freely receiving and freely giving love is not only at the centre of who God is but also flows through all that God has made if we are to believe that what God has made has been birthed in love.

The second image, which Rohr draws out in *The Divine Dance*,[26] is one that I am beautifully aware of. When our son Leo wakes up in the morning, he will often come through to our bedroom and climb in-between me and Bex. He doesn't go back to sleep very often, but just wants to be in this space between us. Rohr describes this simply yet beautifully as 'the space between'. He says, 'They literally rest in the space, the relationship, between you.'[27]

Now the great challenge when speaking about centripetal love is that, while God is drawing all things to himself, that does not mean that all things are divine. We are not drawn into the Godhead – we are not divine. Perhaps, though, what we can say is that we are drawn into that space, that relational space, the relationship in-between. That we can exist, snuggled up within the love of God as Father, Son and Holy Spirit, as children of our heavenly '*Abba*'.

Perhaps what we can say is that we have a space at the table to share in fellowship with the Trinitarian God, and that the very 'shape' of God is expressed as an invitation.

Perhaps this little bucket of sea water expresses something of the ocean contained in this prayer of Jesus which we can marvel at together.

Science and Faith Sing Together

What we have reflected on in this chapter is not simply a conversation in theology but it has been increasingly the conversation, not between faith and science, but the singing of a song by faith and science together. Here is where science and faith are speaking the same language. Quantum physics today speaks in the language of connectedness, that everything in our universe is both 'interdependent and interrelated'.[28] That, in the very fabric of reality as we understand it, there is this relational dynamic stemming from the one who is perfect relationship. That we cannot *be*, or be *known*, unless it is through the reality of relationship:

> It is not our individuality that matters . . . but our person-hood, which is meaningless apart from the relationships that beget and sustain each one of us.[29]

Perhaps Paul was expressing this reality to the people in Athens almost two thousand years ago when he said to them, 'For in him we live and move and have our being.'[30]

It is in our relationship, our belonging to the one who is perfect relationship, and it is in our person-hood, as revealed in the one who is perfect unity and diversity with no tension, that we truly live and can move and can find and have a sense of being.

Again, this is the deep mystery but it is one that we must explore and experience further and deeper. This is where science has something to teach us.

Whenever a question is answered in science, it gives rise to more questions. All it does is just push the mystery further downstream and that's great because it means you are always exploring, always searching for a mystery that is just out of reach.

One of the struggles we have in spirituality and faith – and it's generally true in life too – is that we think we have nailed the answers to the big questions. We think we have 'arrived'. And, even though we have pushed the mystery further downstream, we stay where we are, camped happily celebrating our arrival as the mystery floats further and further away.

It is not that there aren't some things we can say for sure. Of course there are. The fact that there is room for doctrine in expressing who God is does not mean that there is no room for mystery. It is just that our doctrine, as helpful as it is, is the half-pint glass, the lung full of air or the bucket full of sea water within the mystery of God. What we must do is to keep asking the questions, keep exploring, keep journeying, keep being drawn in through the invitation of love that is always flowing out, to find not only a sense of belonging but a space of belonging. To actually belong. O'Murchu reflects, 'Divine belonging is the context in which revelation takes place; all creatures are invited to respond.'[31]

It is in this mystery of belonging to God that we see who God is and where we see who we are as his beloved children.

Know that there is more of God than you can possibly ever know. But know that, at the same time, God makes himself known to you, each and every day, with a deep, beautiful and relational love that draws you deeper in as it flows out for God's own self. That, in this space created for you, is the invitation to belong. To belong in all the ways you need, in all the ways you long for, in all the ways you were made for.

So let the water pour and fill you to overflowing. Breathe in deep lungs-full of air. Fill that bucket from the ocean and stare at it in awe and wonder.

As Paul prayed for the church in Ephesus, may this be our prayer as we end this chapter:

> I pray that you may have the power to comprehend, with all the saints, what is the breadth and length and height and depth, and to know the love of Christ that surpasses knowledge, so that you may be filled with all the fullness of God.[32]

7

What a Wonderful World

*'In your goodness you have made us able to hear
the music of the world . . . A divine song that
sings through all creation.'*[1]

We Are Part of a Good Creation

Have there ever been moments when you were totally trans-
fixed by creation? Where you were caught between watching
on in wonder and that profound sense of connection? I can
think of two moments like that.

The first was when I was travelling around Australia in
2004. Camping out in the Red Centre, where there was very
little artificial light, the stars were amazing. I remember just
lying there, looking up at the sky, with a sense that I was both
looking at a beautiful canvas but at the same time that I was
part of something, connected to something so much deeper
than myself.

The second was on a holiday with Bex to Turkey. We travelled for a week on a gulet along the south coast, and there
was an opportunity to fish over the side of the boat. I decided
that I would try to catch enough fish for all of us to eat that

evening for dinner (I think there were around ten of us). After a whole day of fishing and a lot of waiting, as dinner rapidly approached, I finally realized my goal and caught the last fish. We ate dinner on the top deck of the boat in the Mediterranean sea, chatting with good people, eating good food (which I had caught!), and then the sun started to set. The colour of the sun, combined with the clearness of the water, gave us a spectacular show. The sky turned a beautiful shade of red, and then the sea changed to match it, but with the gentle moving of the water, it looked like fire – like the sea was on fire with the glorious red of the sky. We all stood there and watched it, nobody really saying anything, caught up again in that wonder of gazing upon such a beautiful sight, but also drawn into it in a mysterious way.

Why do we have that response to such beauty within creation?

Firstly, I think it is because we are wired to appreciate beauty. God clearly appreciates beauty, or the world that he has made would not be so richly vibrant or creatively expressive. Whether it is the colours of a kingfisher or the vibrancy of a sunset, the grandeur of the mountains or the flowing majesty of the rivers, clearly God is a God who delights in the beauty of what he has made. We, too, as those who are created in the image and the likeness of God, delight in that same beauty. It is also part of our worship because we know that this beauty is not simply these natural things in themselves but because they have been created and sustained by our creator God. As a wonderful man in my congregation, who is now joining with the music of creation at its source, used to tell me, 'We must worship God in the beauty of holiness, but we must never forget to worship God in the holiness of beauty.'

As I lay and looked up at those stars, and as I saw the sunset set fire to the sea, I can tell you that Frank was right: there is holiness in beauty.

We do not, though, merely look upon this creation as though we are apart from it. We feel that sense of connection, of being drawn in, of belonging to that creation because we ourselves are a part of it. Yes, the Bible tells us that there is something special, something unique, in the way that human beings not only relate to Creator God but also reflect something of his image and likeness; but the Bible also makes clear that we too are creatures. We too are created, and some of the biggest problems we have faced in the world, and with our relationship to the rest of the created world, are when we have lost sight of this truth and seen ourselves as outside, or even above, the world that God has made.

We are part of the world that God has made, and the world that God has made is good. We see that time and time again throughout the Genesis poem. In days one, three, four and five, before we get the familiar refrain 'and it was evening, and it was morning', we hear: 'And God saw that it was good.'[2]

At the end of day six, when God had finished making the heavens and the earth, we see: 'God saw everything that he had made, and indeed, it was very good.'[3]

It is important as we seek to understand how we belong, to know not only that we belong in this world that God has made but that this world is good. It is not perfect, but it is very good.

Norman Wirzba tells us, 'To know how to live presupposes that we know who we are and where we are.'[4] In other words, we cannot hope to know how to live in the world today unless we know who we are and we cannot know who we are unless we know where we are.

If we know that we live within the very good world that God has made, then we know that we ourselves, as part of that, are very good. If this is who we know we are, then we will start to live not only very good lives as those created in God's image and likeness but as those deeply connected to that world. In his book, Wirzba speaks of this as 'creatureliness', and explains, 'By creatureliness I mean a human life that tries to be attuned to God as creator and the world as God's creation.'[5]

If we are to understand how we belong in the world that God has made, then we need to be attuned to the one who is good, who, out of that eternal goodness, has made a good creation. As J. Philip Newell said, 'Goodness is not simply a feature of life; it is the very essence of life.'[6]

It is the essence of life because creation comes from the very womb of God. It is out of God's self, his spoken Word that everything comes into being and is nurtured through that creative process. We can see this in the role the Spirit plays in the creative process in Genesis: 'The Spirit of God was hovering over the waters.'[7]

Robert Alter tells us that 'elsewhere [this] describes an eagle fluttering over its young', which shows us that God's creative process is not merely functional but a nurtured birth of beauty and goodness, of which you and I are a part.

Is that what you think when you look in the mirror? Is that what you think when you wonder how you fit within this world that God has made? That you and I are birthed and nurtured in beauty and goodness. Whatever has gone wrong in the world and in us, fundamentally our innate beauty and goodness is unchanging and true.

There are many people in the world today who feel that they are not deserving of love, of goodness, of a place to belong. I have even heard people say of others, 'they are a waste of space, a good for nothing, not made for this world'. That is not what we see in Genesis. What we see in Genesis is that everything God has made has been formed by his love, birthed and nurtured in beauty and goodness and it is within this space that we find a place to belong within his creation. Each person, as those created in the image and the likeness of God, is deserving of those things. Whatever sin has done to us, whatever the consequences of that choice to choose our own path, we are ultimately created as good, to live within a world that is good.

We can see our part in creation as we look at Scripture. Psalm 104 is a wonderful psalm of God as creator of a good and beautiful creation:

> Bless the LORD, O my soul. O LORD my God, you are very great. You are clothed with honour and majesty, wrapped in light as with a garment. You stretch out the heavens like a tent, you set the beams of your chambers on the waters, you make the clouds your chariot, you ride on the wings of the wind, you make the winds your messengers, fire and flame your ministers. You set the earth on its foundations, so that it shall never be shaken. You cover it with the deep as with a garment; the waters stood above the mountains. At your rebuke they flee; at the sound of your thunder they take to flight. They rose up to the mountains, ran down to the valleys to the place that you appointed for them. You set a boundary that they may not pass, so that they might not again cover the earth.

I have only included the first nine verses here, there are thirty-five in total, and I encourage you perhaps to pause for a moment and to read the psalm for yourself, reflecting on the variety and the vibrancy of all that God has made. This is the world we belong to. God has created us to live within it, to be part of it, to be in-tune with it. What happens, though, when we step out of that belonging space, when we lose our way?

We Have Lost Our Way

One of the great challenges for us as we think about our space to belong within creation, is that we have become disconnected from the world around us. We see ourselves as living in it but not so much a part of it. We feel as though we can use the resources of the earth as we want but without any connection or relationship with that world, which leads to an imbalance or abuse. We have forgotten our ancient call to care for the world and to maintain its balance.

Think for a moment about a key mantra we have been exploring so far. Belonging is the space where I freely receive and give. There is balance in that. The ancient traditions of the world always spoke of balance whether it was yin and yang or 'you reap what you sow'; they understood that, for every taking, there had to be a giving. Newton would later speak of this in terms of physics in his third law of motion saying that 'for every action there is an equal and opposite reaction'. Balance.

However, what we have seen is that we, as human beings, take from the world without always thinking of the cost or without fulfilling the other side of the equation in order to bring balance. Without this balance we cannot belong because, without it, we step outside of the good world that God has made to exist within that balance.

According to a recent article for the Natural History Museum,[8] we over-fish the seas so that we can feed ourselves, which has a dramatic effect on the balance of our oceans. We make this worse when around 66 per cent of the oceans' surface has been affected by the chemicals that run off into them and by plastic pollution.

In an article in May 2018, the then Environmental Editor of the *Guardian* newspaper, Damien Carrington, put it starkly:

The world's 7.6 billion people represent just 0.01% of all living things, according to the study. Yet since the dawn of civilization, humanity has caused the loss of 83% of all wild mammals and half of plants, while livestock kept by humans abounds.[9]

He goes on to give figures that suggest that 80 per cent of marine mammals, 50 per cent of plants and 15 per cent of fish have all been lost as a direct result of the rise of human civilization.

I am not against progress or farming, and I do see myself as part of the problem because I, too, am too often focused on receiving from the natural world rather than giving to it. Robert S. White puts starkly the challenge we face: 'If everyone lived in the same way as we do in the West we would need three whole planets like earth to fuel our habits.'[10]

As a church, we have used the resources of organizations whose job it is to help us to reflect upon our environmental impact and to make changes to restore more balance.[11] It ranges widely: from the toilet paper you buy, to the boiler you use, to how we teach about these themes. We see it very much as a process; we have made some good progress, but we still have a way to go.

This disconnect doesn't just affect the rest of creation around us, it affects us deep down in the core of who we are. Because if we remove ourselves from the good world that God has made, if we unplug from it, then we lose something profound along the way. We lose that sense of being birthed and nurtured in beauty and goodness.

All things are deeply connected. Physics uses the language of a sound that can be heard in all things from the beginnings of the universe. There is a reverberation of God's voice in everything that has been made, a melody that quietly hums in the background of every atom in the cosmos . . . 'it is very good'. This ancient song comes from the dawning of time, but we have forgotten it or stepped too far away to hear it. And the cost has not just been borne by us but by the animals and fish, the rivers and oceans, the forests and mountains.

There is always a challenge here. Like many others, I grew up within a Christianity that was on the one hand keen to protect the world that God has made but, on the other hand, was reluctant to talk about or connect to the natural world and that saw the natural world as kindling for some great end-times divine bonfire.

I remember in a previous church that one of the members of our congregation took me to task after a sermon on caring for creation, saying that 'Jesus died for man not monkeys'. That view will be shared by many even if they would not voice it in such a way. My answer to her at the time is the answer which I still hold true to today and is so beautifully expressed in Colossians 1:

All the broken and dislocated pieces of the universe – people and things, animals and atoms – get properly fixed and fit together in vibrant harmonies, all because of his death, his blood that poured down from the cross.[12]

Jesus has come to redeem all of creation and to restore that which is broken to wholeness. Not only human beings *and* the natural world but human beings *to* the natural world so that we might find our place again within it and belong to the good world that God has made.

This linking together of human beings and creation is rooted in Scripture and highlighted, in particular, by Paul in his letter to the Romans:

The created world itself can hardly wait for what's coming next. Everything in creation is being more or less held back.

God reins it in until both creation and all the creatures are ready and can be released at the same moment into the glorious times ahead. Meanwhile, the joyful anticipation deepens.[13]

The eternal fate of creation and humanity are bound together. We were created as part of creation as a whole, to belong within God's created world. When human beings stepped away from that divine order, we brought a great imbalance to ourselves and creation. And, since that moment, Paul says that creation has been 'groaning'[14] as it waits for us to be brought back into the space of belonging once again.

There are, among all the challenges, signs of genuine hope.

Hold On to Reconnection

During the time of lockdown during the Covid-19 pandemic, there were lots of positive ways in which we began to reconnect again and find our place of belonging within creation.

One of the main things I have thought, and heard other people speaking about often during this time, is birdsong. People say things like 'have you heard how much more the birds are singing?' To be honest, I thought of it in those terms as well. I think, though, that there is much more of a balance in even this seemingly small matter. Because there has been less traffic and less human movement in our cities and neighbourhoods, wildlife is venturing deeper into 'our world' than perhaps before. Yes, the birds may be singing more as a result of this, but it may also be that we are more still, more aware, less distracted than we were before and so more able to notice them when they do sing.

People are taking daily walks who perhaps have not taken daily walks before. People who have spent most of the day in the office are now spending time walking with their families in the green, open spaces of the world.

Scientists now have a word for this time and its impact on the natural world: anthropause. This has been the great pause in human activity, and the effect this pause has had on our planet cannot be ignored. Now the earth is beginning to breathe again. Air pollution is down significantly and water quality has improved. Less pollution in cities means that the stars can be seen more clearly at night and the dawn chorus will continue long past dawn because of less competing noise.

However, will this just be for a little while? Will creation come up for air only for humanity's boot to come down on its throat again when all this 'returns to normal'.

Will you look back nostalgically at the spring and summer of 2020 as the time you heard the birds sing, only to struggle to answer your children's questions about why they don't hear them anymore?

What we are seeing in this season is a re-connection with creation, a realigning to the rhythms and patterns of the world around us. We are seeing the beauty around us, which we are usually too busy to notice.

This connection, though, is fragile; we know that all too well. It will be so easy for us to simply forget and move on. It will be so easy for us to fail to hear the song that buzzes through creation as the traffic drowns it out and the grey of the office blocks mutes its colours. Will we listen to the call of creation to us?

> Life is relational . . . we find well-being in and through one another as an earth community, and not on our own; that we find wholeness in the circle of unity, and not in separation.[15]

So we must not only enjoy that connection but we must protect it. We must nurture it and we must fight for it. Because to lose it would mean we lose a part of who we are; part of that ancient connection to that which is good and beautiful which ultimately reflects a God of goodness and beauty. This is our home, not only in the sense that we physically live here, but in the sense of it being a place of safety and nurture, a defining space, a place to belong. Many have felt that over these months of lockdown, and many know that they can no longer turn their backs on that life.

Freely Give

We have seen that, as Christians, we have both contributed to the problem and the solution, but we cannot allow our theology to continue to contribute to the problem.

In this book, so far, we have looked at belonging as a place where we can freely receive and freely give. We have seen that the world we have been given to live as a part of is very good. It is a beautiful creation which we have received freely from God as our home. However, belonging cannot simply be a place of receiving; it must also be a place where we freely give. So how do we freely give to creation?

In my book *Infused with Life*, I spend some time in the opening chapters speaking about how we too are part of the rhythms of creation and that we have a lot to learn from them in finding rhythm and balance in our own lives. I mention that there is a challenge for us in how we interpret the mandate given to human beings by God in regard to our interactions with the created world.[16]

> Then God said, 'Let us make humankind in our image, according to our likeness; and let them have dominion over the fish of the sea, and over the birds of the air, and over the cattle, and

over all the wild animals of the earth, and over every creeping thing that creeps upon the earth.' So God created humankind in his image, in the image of God he created them; male and female he created them. God blessed them, and God said to them, 'Be fruitful and multiply, and fill the earth and subdue it; and have dominion over the fish of the sea and over the birds of the air and over every living thing that moves upon the earth.' God said, 'See, I have given you every plant yielding seed that is upon the face of all the earth, and every tree with seed in its fruit; you shall have them for food.'[17]

The huge problem that we often have with our theology of caring for creation is that we view words like 'dominion' and 'subdue' outside of the narrative of 'being made in the image of God'. We often fall into the trap of viewing 'being made in the image of God' as something that separates us from creation, allowing us to do what we want with it.

However, we are to look on what God has made through the eyes of one made in his image and to echo his words 'it is good' over that creation, by the way we see it and behave towards it; that this world is beautiful and good and that it needs to be cared for and nurtured.

In that sense, we are not overlords to the rest of creation, but we are tenant farmers and caregivers to a land which ultimately belongs to God.

The Bible does not let us forget that this world is not ours but God's. King David spoke these words over the gathered people:

Blessed are you, O LORD, the God of our ancestor Israel, for ever and ever. Yours, O LORD, are the greatness, the power, the glory, the victory, and the majesty; for all that is in the heavens and on the earth is yours; yours is the kingdom, O LORD, and you are exalted as head above all.[18]

He also spoke of it frequently in Psalms like Psalm 24:

> The earth is the LORD's and all that is in it, the world, and those who live in it; for he has founded it on the seas, and established it on the rivers.[19]

We are part of the world that God has made, but it remains *his* world. How does God treat this world that is his to do with as he pleases? Psalm 145 gives us the answer:

> The LORD is good to all, and his *compassion* is over all that he has made.[20]

If God has compassion on all that he has made, then we too, as those made in his image, should have compassion on it.

I do not often go to Leviticus to get answers to questions. However, there is something striking in Leviticus 25 that sums this up for us:

> The land shall not be sold in perpetuity, for the land is mine; with me you are but aliens and tenants. Throughout the land that you hold, you shall provide for the redemption of the land.[21]

We are tenants on the land that God owns. So our relationship with creation is not that we are above it or owners of it; we are a part of it but given a special mandate to have compassion over it and care for it as those made in the image of God.

God's people were also told here in Leviticus that they were to provide for the redemption of the land. What does it mean to redeem the land? Perhaps it is to care for the land in such a way that it is saved from the destruction it is so easily subjected to by human beings. As we have seen, this call is certainly relevant today for God's people.

I have met Christians who still cringe at language like 'save the planet', and whether that is the language you would choose to use or not, this is very much at the heart of what is being said in Leviticus 25. We are to have compassion for the world that God has made. Compassion for the forests, seas, rivers, fields and air; compassion for the wildlife from the mightiest beast to the things that creep and crawl on the earth. Because this is the world we belong to, because we are a part of it and because it is our role to maintain its beauty and goodness. We take so much from God's creation – the water we drink and the food we eat – and that, in itself, is not wrong at all, especially when done respectfully; but if we truly want to belong, then we also need to be those who restore the balance and give back freely.

The ancient mothers and fathers of our faith spoke about how Christianity had two holy books: a big book and a little book. The little book was the Holy Scriptures, and the big book was creation. They said that in this holy book of creation, God has etched his goodness into every flower, every tree, every plant; that the animals sing his praise in the morning and the evening; that the creatures that dance, leap for joy for their Creator. That God's majesty is inscribed in the stars and painted in the sunset and that all these things speak to us about a God who created a world that is vast and vibrant, beautiful and good.

It is in and to this world, my friends, that you and I belong!

8

Ruth: A Story of the Ordinary

'What are the lengths that we go to in order to belong? What are we prepared to risk?'

An Explosive Start

The Bible is full of dramatic stories. Stories that take your breath away and stretch your imagination. The book of Ruth, though, seems to be a story rooted in ordinariness. However, if there is anything that I have learned in the past few weeks of lockdown during the Covid-19 pandemic, and I know many of you will feel this way too, it is that there is always treasure in the ordinary.

In the days when the judges ruled, there was a famine in the land, and a certain man of Bethlehem in Judah went to live in the country of Moab, he and his wife and two sons. The name of the man was Elimelech and the name of his wife Naomi, and the names of his two sons were Mahlon and Chilion; they were Ephrathites from Bethlehem in Judah. They went into the country of Moab and remained there. But Elimelech, the husband of Naomi, died, and she was left with her two sons. These took Moabite wives; the name of one was Orpah and the name of the other Ruth. When they had lived there for about ten years, both Mahlon and Chilion also died, so that the woman was left without her two sons or her husband.[1]

Here, at the beginning of the book, we are introduced to some of the main characters of the book of Ruth. Central to the story is a small family from the town of Bethlehem, a man named Elimelech and his wife Naomi. There is a famine in the land, and all of a sudden there is no food for them, which seems on the face of things to be ironic because Bethlehem means 'house of bread'; there is nothing to eat in the house of bread. Now this taps into what we have already been exploring in the book. Perhaps, at some point in life, you have unexpectedly found an area lacking that should be a place of abundance – maybe it's a relationship or a job or a place. What is unsettling is that this was meant to be the house of bread, but now it's a place of famine, and the question rises like the grumble from a hungry belly: how can I stay here?

Perhaps your challenge is with God. The name Elimelech means 'God is my King', and yet its seems as though God isn't providing. Perhaps you have been there too? Where it seems as though all that you have known is falling apart, and you have placed your trust in God and he just isn't coming through for you. Perhaps you have experienced something of what this small family from Bethlehem has experienced and know the pain of unanswered prayer, and you, too, know how tempting it is to take matters into your own hands.

For this family, their challenge was a destination: Moab. Moab were the neighbours of Judah but they were also the enemies of Judah. Their god, Chemosh, was a god to whom the people sacrificed children; he was a god of blood. So you can imagine how hard it must have been for a man whose name was 'God is my King' to go to a place like Moab to find food.

Have you ever been in that position? Where you were desperately in need of help but the place you knew could provide that help was the last place that you wanted to go? Perhaps it's not a place at all but a person; the last person that you would ever want to ask for help from and yet you know that they will be the person who can provide it.

While Elimelech and Naomi were living in Moab, their two sons got married to local women. And then tragedy strikes the family. Elimelech dies, and then so do the two sons. So all of a sudden, Naomi is on her own in a foreign land with two local daughters-in-law and grieving the loss of what seems like her entire family. At this time, they had been living in Moab for ten years. When we see in verse 1 that they 'went to live' in that country, the word that is used is more likely the word 'sojourn' or 'visit', which has a much more temporary meaning and leads us to think that their intention was to stay a short while to see out the famine. Now they had been living there for a decade and they are almost settled in the land as Judean ex-pats.

All of this is just in the first five verses of the book of Ruth. So even though this is a story of ordinary people, it also comes with the understanding that the ordinary lives of ordinary people are often full of drama and struggle.

Then she started to return with her daughters-in-law from the country of Moab, for she had heard in the country of Moab that the LORD had had consideration for his people and given them food. So she set out from the place where she had been living, she and her two daughters-in-law, and they went on their way to go back to the land of Judah. But Naomi said to her two daughters-in-law, 'Go back each of you to your mother's house.

May the LORD deal kindly with you, as you have dealt with the dead and with me. The LORD grant that you may find security, each of you in the house of your husband.' Then she kissed them, and they wept aloud. They said to her, 'No, we will return with you to your people.' But Naomi said, 'Turn back, my daughters, why will you go with me? Do I still have sons in my womb that they may become your husbands? Turn back, my daughters, go your way, for I am too old to have a husband. Even if I thought there was hope for me, even if I should have a husband tonight and bear sons, would you then wait until they were grown? Would you then refrain from marrying? No, my daughters, it has been far more bitter for me than for you, because the hand of the LORD has turned against me.' Then they wept aloud again. Orpah kissed her mother-in-law, but Ruth clung to her. So she said, 'See, your sister-in-law has gone back to her people and to her gods; return after your sister-in-law.' But Ruth said, 'Do not press me to leave you or to turn back from following you! Where you go, I will go; where you lodge, I will lodge; your people shall be my people, and your God my God. Where you die, I will die – there will I be buried. May the LORD do thus and so to me, and more as well, if even death parts me from you!' When Naomi saw that she was determined to go with her, she said no more to her.[2]

The story continues as Naomi, Orpah and Ruth leave Moab. In verse 6, we read that the reason for the return was because the '*LORD had had consideration for his people* and given them bread'. Now, for those who are familiar with the Jewish story, this phrase may cause you to sit up and take notice. Way back in Exodus chapter three, when Moses heard God speaking out of the burning bush, this is what God said to Moses:

I have observed the misery of my people who are in Egypt; I have heard their cry on account of their taskmasters. Indeed, I know their sufferings, and I have come down to deliver them . . .[3]

You see the people of God, of whom Naomi was a part, knew what it meant when the Lord has consideration for the plight of his people. It meant rescue. It meant freedom. It meant moving out of the foreign lands where other gods were worshipped and into a land where they could live in the protection and the provision of the Lord. This is the story that runs right the way through the Bible, and time and time again we see the little town where Naomi, Ruth and Orpah are headed, right at the centre: Bethlehem.

So Naomi sets off on the journey home because, for her, that sense of belonging she feels is to the place she had once called home. On face value, we could assume that, before the death of her husband and sons, her sense of belonging was to her family. After all, she leaves her home and all that she has known to go with Elimelech and her sons to Moab when the famine hits. Now that they have gone, she clings to the other thing that gives her a sense of belonging: place. We see that time and again in the Bible. We see it with Peter after the crucifixion and resurrection of Jesus. Peter goes back to the place and the past-time that he knows: 'I am going fishing.'[4] It seems that in times of upheaval and uncertainty, many of us revert to what we know.

On the journey, she tells her two daughters-in-law to leave her. In essence, she has nothing for them now. Everything that bound these two young Moabite women to Naomi was gone. In every cultural, legal and religious sense, there was now no bond that held them together, except perhaps the bond they shared in their grief. Naomi blesses them for the kindness that they have shown her, that they might have the blessing of comfort and security and love again where they had experienced loss. It is a beautiful blessing, not a shun. Naomi cares for these women, but she is acutely aware, as we shall see, that she is returning home a very different woman than when she left.

Orpah decides to head home, but Ruth decides to stay and argue her case with Naomi in what is one of the most moving exchanges in Scripture. It is easy to get caught up in the beauty of this exchange and miss what Ruth is actually claiming here, which is far deeper than mere sentiment. What it shows us is that our roots of belonging, whatever they may be, are far more than sentiment; they are often roots which define us more deeply than we know.

Let's look at the claims Ruth makes for a moment.

Where you go, I will go; where you lodge, I will lodge . . .

This is a claim to land. Land was important for the people of God, as it was the land that God had provided and set apart for them. If we look back to Deuteronomy, we catch a glimpse of that:

But he brought us out from there to bring us in and give us the land he promised on oath to our ancestors.[5]

In the same way that God had brought his people out of the land of Egypt, God was drawing out Naomi – and through her, Ruth – from the land of Moab. In the same way that God's bringing out of his people was in order to bring them into his promises, God draws Naomi and Ruth out in order that he might bring them into his promises.

However, the word that Ruth uses is deeper and far more telling than simply claiming a white picket fence in a nice Bethlehem suburb. The Hebrew word '*lun*', which we have translated as 'lodge', is far more temporary.[6] It is about travelling and wandering. So while it is a claim to land, that land is personal as it is whatever land Naomi finds herself on, however temporary. How often is that true for our sense of belonging, too, when it comes to land. If I think about my own life since I have been in ministry, I can certainly empathize with Ruth's sentiment and claim. Since Bex and I married during our time in Bible college, we have moved four times and lived in four different houses. In each of those houses, we have made a home in the time we have lived there, but it was not the physical land or the house itself that made it home: it was Bex and, latterly, Leo. They have been my sense of home, and they make the space we live in a place of belonging. For sure, we need a space, but that space would be nothing without them. So, for Ruth, that claim to land was not just to any old land but to belong in the same space as Naomi, however transient or precarious that land was.

> Your people shall be my people, and your God my God.

This is a claim to tribe, but one which goes far beyond Naomi. As we have already seen, when her husband died, Ruth's family link with Naomi effectively ended. Ruth could have claimed a place back within that family, but she realizes that, by joining herself to Naomi, she is also taking on Naomi's people and all that this meant.

Naomi's people had an identity that went far beyond tribe.
They were the people of Israel, and Israel was far more than
land. They were the children of Abraham, Isaac and Jacob
(Israel). They were the heirs of the promise that had brought
them about and brought them in. They were the descendants
of the generation that had walked through the sea, who had
followed the fiery pillar, who had seen the walls of Jericho fall.
This was not simply any people; they were Yahweh's people.

So, for Ruth, belonging to Naomi's people meant also to
belong to Naomi's God. Ruth must have seen something in
Naomi in those years in Moab that led her to believe that following Naomi's God was a good idea. Perhaps, though, as with
all else we have seen in these opening chapters of Ruth, it went
deeper than that too.

When Ruth married Elimelech and Naomi's son, she was
drawn into the people of God through that marriage. She became an inheritor of the promises of the people of God. However, when her husband died, that was taken away from her.
In this emotional and moving pledge to Naomi, we see Ruth
clinging on to that promise – even the hope of that promise –
with all she has. She has tasted and seen that the Lord is
good, but now that she has, she will not let go. Much like the
name-sake of the people she has promised to belong to, it's as
if she is saying, 'I will not let go until you bless me.'[7] If it was
that clinging, that wrestling that transformed Jacob into Israel,
perhaps it was in this act of clinging, a refusal to let go, that
Ruth is brought into that same spiritual heritage. Here, Ruth
shows just how 'Israel' she is.

In that way, she is similar to Tamar in Genesis 38. She too
had been part of the family of God's people; Jacob was her
grandfather-in-law. She too found herself potentially on the
outside of the people of promise; taking matters into her own

hands, she wrote herself back into the story. Her child, Perez, which means 'breakthrough' is mentioned at the end of Ruth:

> May your house be like the house of Perez, whom Tamar bore to Judah, because of the offspring which the LORD will give you from this young woman.[8]

Both Ruth and Tamar wrote themselves back into the story of the people of God from the outside. They too had experienced what it was to belong, and when faced with the threat of losing that, decided to risk everything in order to keep hold of the blessing.

What are the lengths that we go to in order to belong? What are we prepared to risk? Rejection is a very real fear for many of us when we come to seek a space to belong. We have already explored that together, but we see it again in both the story of Ruth and that of Tamar. There comes a moment in both stories where the fate of both hangs on the decision of one person who has the power to cast them away or to embrace them into the space of belonging. Both women show incredible bravery in risking that rejection in order to cling on to the promise and to belong within it.

Our search for belonging might take us away from what is comfortable. We might ask ourselves why we would be prepared to leave the security of what we have to journey into the unknown. Why would we be prepared to leave the old tribal loyalties to search for a place to belong? For many looking on, these choices might seem rash or irresponsible, but when the heart calls, when it recognizes its own depths in another place, then that call is unmistakeable and the choice becomes very simple. Not simply a matter of stay or go, but a matter of live or die. When you view it in those terms, you can understand why it is worth the risk.

For Ruth, she risks being a woman on her own, in a patri-
archal world, with no protection. She leaves behind all that
she has known to bind herself to a woman who is bitter and
has made it clear that she has nothing for her. What a risk. We
aren't even told by the writer why Ruth would do something
like this other than what we can read from this encounter, and
perhaps we know from our experience that this is the strength
of the desire to belong; that we are prepared to risk whatever it
takes to hang on to it.

A Story to Cross Borders

As we have already seen, Ruth is a story that crosses borders.
What is interesting is that, as soon as Naomi and Ruth return
home to Bethlehem, Ruth is referred to as 'Ruth the Moabite'.[9]
Even though she is now in the land she has adopted as her own
through Naomi, she is still very much on the outside.

Here we see the story continue:

Now Naomi had a kinsman on her husband's side, a prominent
rich man, of the family of Elimelech, whose name was Boaz.
And Ruth the Moabite said to Naomi, 'Let me go to the field
and glean among the ears of grain, behind someone in whose
sight I may find favour.' She said to her, 'Go, my daughter.' So
she went. She came and gleaned in the field behind the reapers.
As it happened, she came to the part of the field belonging to
Boaz, who was of the family of Elimelech. Just then Boaz came
from Bethlehem. He said to the reapers, 'The LORD be with
you.' They answered, 'The LORD bless you.' Then Boaz said to
his servant who was in charge of the reapers, 'To whom does
this young woman belong?' The servant who was in charge of

the reapers answered, 'She is the Moabite who came back with Naomi from the country of Moab. She said, "Please let me glean and gather among the sheaves behind the reapers." So she came, and she has been on her feet from early this morning until now, without resting even for a moment.'[10]

Now, we need to understand something of the legal background of the day in order to understand the significance of what is going on here because letting Ruth glean in his field is far more than just a random act of kindness from Boaz. It is a response rooted in the gracious provision of God through Torah.

We read about it in Deuteronomy 24:

When you are harvesting in your field and you overlook a sheaf, do not go back to get it. Leave it for the foreigner, the fatherless and the widow, so that the LORD your God may bless you in all the work of your hands. When you beat the olives from your trees, do not go over the branches a second time. Leave what remains for the foreigner, the fatherless and the widow. When you harvest the grapes in your vineyard, do not go over the vines again. Leave what remains for the foreigner, the fatherless and the widow. Remember that you were slaves in Egypt. That is why I command you to do this.[11]

This practice happened every harvest as a provision for those who might get forgotten by the system. It was a means of provision for the most vulnerable in society.

There was also extra provision given every three years which we read about earlier in Deuteronomy 14:

At the end of every three years, bring all the tithes of that year's produce and store it in your towns, so that the Levites (who have no land allotted to them or inheritance of their own) and the foreigners, the fatherless and the widows who live in your towns may come and eat and be satisfied, and so that the LORD your God may bless you in all the work of your hands.[12]

So why is it that God's people are called to do this? Because it is who God himself is. We see that in the specific conditions of Leviticus 19:

When you reap the harvest of your land, do not reap to the very edges of your field or gather the gleanings of your harvest. Do not go over your vineyard a second time or pick up the grapes that have fallen. Leave them for the poor and the foreigner. I am the LORD your God.[13]

It is because of who God is, because of how generous and open his heart is, that his people are to provide for the poor and the foreigner. It is because 'He defends the cause of the fatherless and the widow, and loves the foreigner residing among you, giving them food and clothing',[14] that his people are called to do the same.

What is so challenging to us in our modern-day culture is that this provision is not charitable but written into the very law that governs them. That built into the framework of the society that they lived in was a provision for the most vulnerable, hungry, powerless and unprotected people among them. This was no small matter to them. The challenge comes in that it should not be for us either. David Atkinson, in his commentary on Ruth, challenges us in our priorities:

A concern for the just distribution of earth's resources is no soft option for Christian people. It is part of the meaning of belonging to the covenant people of God.[15]

The concept of Jubilee is also central to these practices. That every fiftieth year, all debts were cancelled, all slaves released and all land returned to their original owners.

If I think about the vulnerable I see every week in our church, I wonder how our society has affected them.

On the lower floor of our church building is the city homeless shelter, which is run by the charity Julian House. There are thirty beds in the hostel and some fantastic staff who give their time and their energy to engage with and care for some of the most chaotic and vulnerable people in our society. What does it mean for our homeless community to find a place to belong?

On a Tuesday lunchtime, we host a group from 'Bath Welcomes Refugees', who come alongside mainly Syrian refugees who have relocated to Bath. I have heard some of the stories of what these people have left behind in war-torn Syria, and how they are being cared for and supported as they transition into a new culture and a new life. What does it mean for our refugees to find a place to belong?

Every single day, in our church café, Bath Foodbank meets and provides for those who are hungry and have little or no food. Not only do they provide this service for them but they have a cup of coffee with them and talk to them as human beings, showing them respect and dignity. The fact that we give away over one thousand cups of coffee each year in this process shows you how big a challenge this is, even in a small city like Bath. What does it mean for our hungry to find a place to belong?

Last year, we were delighted to partner – along with Holy Trinity Combe Down, another church in Bath – with Christians Against Poverty, a charity that exists because 'nobody should be held hostage by debt and poverty'. We were working with people in the city who have become imprisoned by debt, and working with them in order to set them free. What does it mean for our poor to find a place to belong?

These are the people who have been failed by our society. I know there are choices that people have made that haven't helped them or that have contributed to the position they find themselves in. I get it – I speak to people in that position every week. Let's be realistic, though; the system we live in isn't stacked in their favour. If I think about the homeless shelter for a moment, around 90 per cent of the service users there have some form of mental health challenge. They cannot get access to the mental health support that perhaps you and I could because, in order to get that support, they need to be in a stable environment, and the hostel is not deemed as a stable environment. Do you see what I mean when I say that the system isn't stacked in their favour?

Are our systems tilted towards the needs of the poor and vulnerable in our society?

Dare we allow ourselves to dream what it would look like in our society if, written into our law, into the very fabric of our culture, was not only the provision for those who were in need but the welcome; the creation of a space to belong. God doesn't just provide through his people for the foreigner and the fatherless, but he loves them. What would it look like in our nation if we saw that at the centre of who we sought to be? As the people of God, this is the work we are called to, to be obedient to it and to be proactive in it.

In his challenging book *A Place at the Table*, Chris Seay reminds us:

> As Christians who are called to love the least of these, we need
> to realize that poverty is not just a problem, it is our problem.[16]

How we own and engage with this problem will not only go some way to solving the great challenges of our society but it will, in the very act of doing it, begin to carve out a space within our society for all to belong and where all can be loved.

The Kinsman Redeemer

We come to the end of the story of Ruth.

> Then Boaz said to the elders and all the people, 'Today you are witnesses that I have acquired from the hand of Naomi all that belonged to Elimelech and all that belonged to Chilion and Mahlon. I have also acquired Ruth the Moabite, the wife of Mahlon, to be my wife, to maintain the dead man's name on his inheritance, in order that the name of the dead may not be cut off from his kindred and from the gate of his native place; today you are witnesses.' Then all the people who were at the gate, along with the elders, said, 'We are witnesses. May the LORD make the woman who is coming into your house like Rachel and Leah, who together built up the house of Israel. May you produce children in Ephrathah and bestow a name in Bethlehem; and, through the children that the LORD will give you by this young woman, may your house be like the house of Perez, whom Tamar bore to Judah.'[17]

The role of the kinsman redeemer was that, when a male member of the family died, they would assume governance of the dead man's land and take care of the man's family so that they would not be destitute. This also meant that the family line would be continued. Here we see Boaz, who is from the same family as Elimelech, take on responsibility for all his lands and the lands and family of his son Mahlon, which includes his widow Ruth.

Here we have Ruth, the foreigner, the widow, the vulnerable, finding a space to belong within the people of promise. Her precarious journey has led her to this moment. She is far from a victim in the story but one who desires that space to belong so much that she continually writes herself into the story, driving it along.

There are times when we have to do that. Where a place of belonging doesn't automatically come or when circumstances take it from us, then we may need to pursue it. We can take encouragement from Ruth here because in the end comes the blessing of finding that space.

It might be rough along the way. There might be times when we have to hold onto that blessing with everything that we have and hope that we hang on long enough to reach the blessing. What we can see from Ruth is that the blessing of belonging is one that cements her place within the much bigger story.

This is not simply a love story with a happy ending. This is a story of ordinary women and men that is caught up in the greater story of God's purpose and plan. Ruth and Boaz had a son, and they called him Obed; 'he became the father of Jesse, the father of David'.[18]

Ruth became the great-grandmother of King David, and many generations later, another redeemer would be born in the little town of Bethlehem, in the family of Ruth and from the tribe of Judah. He is the one in whom 'all the broken and dislocated pieces of the universe – people and things, animals and atoms – get properly fixed and fit together in vibrant harmonies . . .'[19] He, like Boaz, will pay the price to win you back, to bring you in, to give you a home and a future.

This is a story of what it takes and means to belong and the journey it takes to get there. I pray that in your own journey you may keep writing your story until you find that place to belong. When you do, hold on to it tight, don't let go, and enjoy the blessing.

9

The Great Revealing

'To belong to him is to belong to the New Covenant community . . . no longer confined to the genetic descent . . . nor the rewards of earth, but it is as wide as the cosmos and as eternal as only God's heaven can be.'[1]

What are the popular stories that your family tells about you from when you were young? One of the stories my mum has often told me was an occasion when I was having some difficulty going to bed. I was about seven years old at the time and, according to her, was usually very good at going to bed. However, on this occasion she had to come up a couple of times to tell me that it was time to turn out my light and go to sleep because I was still sat up reading. She tells me that she didn't really pay too much attention to what I was reading on that occasion.

When she heard footsteps she came to the foot of the stairs and called up, 'Andrew, will you please get into bed!' To which the reply came down, 'But the problem is, Mummy, I'm having a bit of trouble understanding Revelation.'

My mum tried her best to keep a straight face. My dad was cracking up in the lounge. Mum came up and tucked me in and said, 'We'll talk about Revelation in the morning!'

To be honest, I think that was sound advice. We'll talk about Revelation in the morning. Because most of us, if we are honest, struggle with Revelation. Twenty-nine years later I am still struggling with it. So we put it off, or we move on, or we close our eyes and desperately hope to fall asleep as quickly as possible.

A Strange Letter

Hidden in this letter, which brings Scripture to a close, are some of the most precious and significant words in the whole Bible. The problem is that they are hidden within and around all this imagery which is a million miles away from anything we can understand or relate to.

In that sense, Revelation operates on two levels or, at least, in two parts. Firstly you have the specifics. As Rob Bells writes:

> The book of Revelation is a letter. It's written by a pastor named John to his congregation. His people were facing very difficult challenges, and John writes to them to encourage them to stay strong and keep going.[2]

Here we have a disciple of Jesus speaking to real people who are living in the real world, with real challenges, and he wants them to know certain things about the realities they are facing today. That's an important point to make because so often we think of Revelation as something that purely speaks to us about what is going to happen when the world as we know it comes to an end.

This wrapping up of all that we know, the world and life as we know it, is the second level or the second part. Revelation does speak a lot about what happens when the world as we know it comes to an end. There is imagery of heaven, of judgement, of restoration, of justice. There are pictures of heavenly creatures and angels and devils along with all kinds of polemic, political and satirical language. Why is John giving us this information? Is it just to satisfy our curiosity? Is it to simply let us know what is going to happen? No. These words are given to us in order to encourage us and to strengthen us and to give us hope that is meant to help us live today.

Revelation gives us a prophetic glimpse of what will be, in order to help us to live now.

Up until the fourteenth century, there wasn't a book of Revelation. The Bible ended with 'The Apocalypse'. Now that word has all sorts of connotations for us because we have read Revelation. When I think of the word 'apocalypse', I think of the four horsemen, of chaos and panic and fear, of destruction. I think if you were to ask most people whether they thought 'apocalypse' was a word that had good or bad connotations then most people would happily leap to the bad side of the fence.

When the Covid-19 lockdown began in March, in those very early days when you could only leave the house to exercise once a day and to shop for food once a week, there was nothing really on the roads. I could walk down one of the busiest streets in the city where I live, and there would be no cars. Travelling around the city was strange like that, and there were times when it felt as though we were living in some apocalyptic movie. I'm sure that people who worked in airports, shopping centres or other places which normally would be bustling with people, in those early days, would have felt the same.

If you go to where all definitions should be found, the internet, then this is the common answer on most search engines when you type the words 'apocalypse meaning':

1. The complete final destruction of the world, as described in the biblical book of Revelation.

2. An event involving destruction or damage on a catastrophic scale.

I think most people, if you were to ask them about 'The Apocalypse' would give you the same answer.

The thing is, that's not what it means. That's how it is interpreted, but that isn't what the word means. The word comes from two Greek words: the word '*apo*' which means away or after, and the word '*kalupto*' which means to cover or hide. So the word 'apocalypse' means to uncover or reveal. That's how we get our word 'revelation'. In that sense, the meaning behind the letter is to reveal or uncover certain truths and realities that have been hidden, but in that revealing, our lives now are impacted because of it.

Think of it like this. You might reveal the destination of a family holiday to your children in advance because you want them to be excited that you are going. You aren't there yet. It might be weeks or months away. However, your revealing isn't simply to pass them information. It is because you know that this revelation will do something to them in this moment. The holiday is coming, but it still does something in this moment.

Every Tribe, Every People, Every Nation

After this I looked, and there was a great multitude that no one could count, from every nation, from all tribes and peoples and languages, standing before the throne and before the Lamb, robed in white, with palm branches in their hands. They cried out in a loud voice, saying, 'Salvation belongs to our God who is seated on the throne, and to the Lamb!' And all the angels stood around the throne and around the elders and the four living creatures, and they fell on their faces before the throne and worshipped God, singing, 'Amen! Blessing and glory and wisdom and thanksgiving and honour and power and might be to our God for ever and ever! Amen.'[3]

We have this scene in heaven with an uncountable number of people. Here we have the fulfilment of the promise made to Abraham all the way back in the first book of the Bible, Genesis.

He took him [Abram] outside and said, 'Look up at the sky and count the stars – if indeed you can count them.' Then he said to him, 'So shall your offspring be.'[4]

A group of people so numerous that no one can count, like the stars. People from 'every nation, from all tribes and peoples and languages'. Tribalism has no place here. Nationalism has no place here. Ethnicity has no place here . . . because all have a place here. All are included and brought in. No one is excluded.

I have been deeply saddened by the events that have taken place in the United States following the death of George Floyd. For those of you who do not know, George Floyd was an African-American man who was arrested for allegedly using a suspected fake $20 bill to pay for a pack of cigarettes. During his arrest, he was restrained, hands cuffed behind his back. Then a white police officer knelt on his neck, ignoring his pleas to let him breathe, his cries that he could not breathe, and kept kneeling on his neck until he died. The official autopsy revealed that George Floyd was murdered.

The civil unrest that has taken place as a result of this has been seen time and time again, far too many times following the murder of an African-American at the hands of white police officers. Racism has a long, deep history within America, and we can only add our voices to the cries for justice, add our prayers to the prayers for healing and add our efforts to building a just and equal society where the colour of a person's skin does not matter.

The church has not always spoken out against racism in the world and, at times, has actively perpetuated a cycle of injustice and oppression. Nick Page highlights that, in America in the nineteenth century, 'services were generally seen as ways of controlling the slaves, endorsing the status quo and preaching the virtues of obedience'.[5]

However, the church has an important role to play in helping to forge a society where all are welcome and where all belong, regardless of their nation, tribe, people or language. When the church does this, it is actively reflecting not just the world as it should be now but the world as it will be when God has restored all things through Christ.

Recently, I joined a protest against racism in the centre of Bath in affirmation that, while all lives matter, it is important to affirm that black lives matter, especially in the face of the level of racism so many are facing around the world and here in the United Kingdom.

While I was at the protest, I looked around and saw people from different nations, speaking different languages, from different tribes and different skin colours. They had come together because they believed the truth that is the destination and goal that Revelation speaks about: that all lives matter, that all have a place to belong because all are created in the image of God and bear the divine spark within them. To affirm anything else is not only racism but deeply unbiblical. Sadly, though, there are those who use the Bible as a justification for world views that are very far from the heart of God.

The apostle Paul wrote:

> There is no longer Jew or Greek, there is no longer slave or free, there is no longer male and female; for all of you are one in Christ Jesus.[6]

In Christ the old barriers that meant certain people were automatically considered 'in' and others were automatically considered 'out', have been broken down. Now, in Christ all are invited and welcomed and embraced. All are equal.

When the future kingdom that is promised becomes our present reality, there will be a healing that takes place where all the fragmentation that has existed within the human family up to this moment is put right, and the beautiful diversity of humanity will shine in the light of the very presence of God himself.

> The promise of the kingdom of God in which all things attain to right, to life, to peace, to freedom, and to truth, is not exclusive, but inclusive. And so, too, its love, its neighbourliness and its sympathy are inclusive, excluding nothing, but embracing in hope everything wherein God will be all in all.[7]

Creation Made Whole (Again)

> Then the angel showed me the river of the water of life, bright as crystal, flowing from the throne of God and of the Lamb through the middle of the street of the city. On either side of the river is the tree of life with its twelve kinds of fruit, producing its fruit each month; and the leaves of the tree are for the healing of the nations. Nothing accursed will be found there anymore. But the throne of God and of the Lamb will be in

it, and his servants will worship him; they will see his face, and his name will be on their foreheads. And there will be no more night; they need no light of lamp or sun, for the Lord God will be their light, and they will reign for ever and ever.[8]

A couple of chapters ago, we looked at finding our place to belong within creation. About half way through the chapter, I quoted a passage from Romans 8 in *The Message*, which spoke about how our future and the future of creation were linked together because we are part of that creation. The future that awaits for both human beings and the rest of creation is not one of disconnection. Human beings are not simply whisked away up into the clouds to enjoy life all dressed in white while the rest of creation is destroyed. The goal was always for recreation, or a new creation. We see that back in Isaiah 65:

For I am about to create new heavens and a new earth; the former things shall not be remembered or come to mind.[9]

That theme is carried on and expressed in the New Testament when we come to Peter's writing:

But do not ignore this one fact, beloved, that with the Lord one day is like a thousand years, and a thousand years are like one day. The Lord is not slow about his promise, as some think of slowness, but is patient with you, not wanting any to perish, but all to come to repentance. But the day of the Lord will come like a thief, and then the heavens will pass away with a loud noise, and the elements will be dissolved with fire, and the earth and everything that is done on it will be disclosed. Since all these things are to be dissolved in this way, what sort of people ought you to be in leading lives of holiness and godliness, waiting for and hastening the coming of the day of God, because of which the heavens will be set ablaze and dissolved, and the elements will melt with fire? But, in accordance with his promise, we wait for new heavens and a new earth, where righteousness is at home.[10]

It might seem as we read through these words of Peter that the end result for creation is to be destroyed by fire. After all, that is what it seems to say here. However, fire is not always meant to mean destruction, and not all destruction is bad.

Take for example how you refine a precious metal. Through fire. That has to do with purification and not destruction. When we sing words like 'purify my heart' in worship, or speak of the refiner's fire, we are not asking God to destroy our hearts. Far from it. What we are asking is that God would allow his holy fire to burn away all that is not good within our hearts so that what remains is good and pure. In praying that, we are speaking of our belief that fire does not always mean destruction, but also that not all destruction is bad because what is destroyed in that process are the impurities that do not have a place within that precious metal.

So it is with the new creation, or the recreation. The fire that is coming is not about destruction but about renewal and recreation. That God's holy fire will remove from the creation all the impurities that exist within it, and through this refining fire, he will bring all things back into his 'very good'[11] purpose.

Verse 10 of the above passage in 2 Peter 3 originally said:

But the day of the Lord will come as a thief in the night; in which the heavens shall pass away with a great noise, and the elements shall melt with fervent heat, the earth also and the works that are therein *shall be burned up*.[12]

It is interesting that, while the King James Version ends verse 10 with 'shall be burned up', the NRSV translates it 'will be disclosed'. Ruth Valerio describes how the word that is translated as 'burned up' by the KJV should better be translated 'will be found'.[13] So, in that sense, there is a similar theme with what we have already explored with apocalypse being about uncovering or revelation. This word from where Peter gets 'will be found' is where we get the word 'eureka'.

Ruth Valero goes on to say:

> What is being said here, therefore, is not that the eschatological fire will come to destroy the earth, but that it will come to purify the earth so that what is bad will be burnt up, and what is good will be left.[14]

This is exciting because, with those imperfections removed, it reveals to us who we really are. So with the imperfections of sin and decay removed from creation, it reveals our identity which is a reason to celebrate, not be fearful. As Rob Bell puts it:

> When the writers of the Bible wrote about this laying bare, it was with the anticipation of everything being made right, put back in place, restored. It was a hopeful, buoyant, joyous expectation that there is still a better future for the world.[15]

There will come a restoring of all things, and a recreating of all things when the kingdom in all its fullness is revealed. There will also be the healing of the broken relationship between humanity and creation.

God created the world as very good, but human beings chose to live outside of that goodness and to choose their own path. This did not just have an effect on humanity but creation too.

We brought an element of decay into creation, and when God renews the whole of creation through his purifying fire, this relationship between humanity and creation will be restored along with it.

Then, together, united once again as creatures of our God and King, we can sing our praises as those who belong to him and to one another.

Face-to-Face Restoration

> Then I saw a new heaven and a new earth; for the first heaven and the first earth had passed away, and the sea was no more. And I saw the holy city, the new Jerusalem, coming down out of heaven from God, prepared as a bride adorned for her husband. And I heard a loud voice from the throne saying, 'See, the home of God is among mortals. He will dwell with them; they will be his peoples, and God himself will be with them; he will wipe every tear from their eyes. Death will be no more; mourning and crying and pain will be no more, for the first things have passed away.' And the one who was seated on the throne said, 'See, I am making all things new.' Also he said, 'Write this, for these words are trustworthy and true.'[16]

So we have seen how God at the end will remove the dividing walls between us, and how he will heal the relationship between humanity and creation. There is also a great work of restored relationship between human beings and God himself.

You see, the great work of salvation that has been brought about through Jesus is complete. It is complete in the sense that everything that needs to be done in order to restore that relationship has been done. There is no need for God to do anything more because what Jesus did was complete, and as he himself said on the cross, 'It is finished.' However, we are painfully aware at times that in spite of that finished work, we do not live in a reality which has caught on to that completion. There is a time yet to come, a reality yet experienced, where God will, through Christ, bring reality in line with that work of the cross and the empty tomb.

Our relationship with God and with each other is still affected by sin; we are still subject to death and we are still so often clothed with that false self which robs us of knowing who we truly are.

What we hope for is to be free from sin, to be free from death and to be clothed with the fullness of who we have been created to be. The good news is that we can experience all that today through Jesus but in a limited way because we still live in a reality where the fulfilment of God's promise has yet to be revealed.

Paul understood that hope and longing, and he expressed it in his first letter to the church in Corinth:

> For now we see in a mirror, dimly, but then we will see face to face. Now I know only in part; then I will know fully, even as I have been fully known.[17]

We know the first reality: everything we know about ourselves after years of self-reflection; everything we have come to understand and express about God; all the intimate moments with God in prayer, worship or walking in his creation – all the best of these and more are like looking through a dark glass or into a dirty mirror. That is not to downplay them at all but to highlight just how much better life is going to be when the fullness of God's kingdom is revealed.

Then we will see face to face. I think sometimes we lose the impact of the words of the Bible because we become so familiar with them. Just let that sink in for a moment. The God you have prayed to, worshipped, trusted in, hoped and lived for is a God you have never seen with your own eyes. However, a day is coming when you will stand face to face before God. Face to face! Despite all you do not know about God, about yourself, about the world; then you will know fully, in the same way as you are fully known.

Here is a work of recreation. It is new, but it is not unfamiliar; that is, it is in line with what God has always been doing. Way back in Genesis 1, God created human beings as a part of a world that God has made. Those human beings enjoy relationship with each other, with creation and with God. God walked in the garden with human beings. God shared the space with his creation. The first creation was always meant to be a harmony where all that God had made lived in intimate relationship with him.

So, this new creation expresses that same desire of God to be with that which God loves.

What is important to highlight here is that this eternal place of belonging isn't a place of divine download where we will simply know more about God, more about ourselves and more about the world. We are questioning beings, and many of us have questions which we feel would be the first things that we would ask when we get to heaven. I know that I do.

This eternal space of belonging is one of relationship in its fullest, deepest and most vibrant kind. It is full, free, alive, animated and joyous. It is not a place of merely enlightenment but a place of belonging, body, mind and soul.

As David Bentley Hart reminds us about this Divine Victory:

Rather than showing us how the tears of a small girl suffering in the dark were necessary for the building of the Kingdom, he will instead raise her up and wipe away all tears from her eyes – and there shall be no more death, nor sorrow, nor crying, nor pain, for the former things will have passed away, and he who sits on the throne will say, 'Behold, I make all things new.'[18]

These words are some of the most moving I have read because they connect with something deep down inside of me: not a desire to know answers to the deep questions I have (and trust me, I have many), but the desire to be scooped up in the arms of my heavenly Father and to let him wipe away the tears in my eyes.

Think back to where we have journeyed together. If you have shed tears because you have ever felt as though you don't belong or because that search to belong has been long and hard and painful, it is in the arms of the one who is perfect and unchanging eternal love that you will find those tears wiped away. Where you can rest, and breathe in his arms, knowing you are safe, knowing you are home, knowing you are known. It is here that we were made to belong.

What does it look like to freely receive and freely give within this restored relationship? Everything! To freely give of yourself, the essence of who you are as beloved, created in beauty and goodness. What purer form of giving can there be? Who could give more?

The wonder is that this is also how we receive. The God who created stars, who forged the mountains, who spoke matter into being, gives freely to us the essence of who he is. That is what we are called to receive: to receive the face-to-face fullness of the God who is love and to let it radiate through our very souls with an eternal glow. Who wants a harp when that's on offer?

Belonging is Going Somewhere

So how do we fit this in with what we have been exploring in terms of belonging? What Revelation reveals to us is that our sense of belonging isn't static, but it is going somewhere. We are all searching for ways to belong and places to belong to. Joseph Myers says:

> The search for community is a fundamental life search. We need to belong. We search with some increasing desperation as terms such as 'neighbour', 'family', and 'congregation' are being redefined. People are searching to belong in new places and through new experiences.[19]

The reason, perhaps, why we keep searching is because, in a very real sense, those places of belonging never fully arrive. What we get are glimpses of belonging in our lives, ourselves, through church, in family and in creation. However beautiful and secure they are, they remain glimpses because belonging isn't static. We don't find a space to belong and then hope it stays like that forever, because people and dynamics change. We change.

Belonging is a journey, and a journey we take together throughout our lives. It twists and turns, goes up and down. On this road you can have companions or you can feel very lonely.

What we are journeying towards, though, is an uncovering, a revealing of what true belonging really is, the belonging we have been searching and waiting for. In this true belonging, all our places of belonging find their fulfilment. Paul talks about our resurrection to this true belonging in his second letter to the church in Corinth:

> Compared to what's coming, living conditions around here seem like a stopover in an unfurnished shack, and we're tired of it! We've been given a glimpse of the real thing, our true home, our resurrection bodies! The Spirit of God whets our appetite by giving us a taste of what's ahead. He puts a little of heaven in our hearts so that we'll never settle for less.[20]

What is revealed to us, in the end, is that everything we have searched for will be swallowed up into life. Death is not the end of belonging. As Charles Spurgeon said, God has turned the grave into a bed and death into merely sleep.[21] What we are destined for, our home, is life. Full, free and glorious life; for all creation, for you and me, in the very presence of God himself.

We have come to the end of our journey together in this book, but in all the ways that matter, the real journey goes on. The search to belong is deep within us because it was something we were made for. You and I were not simply created to exist or to co-exist, we were made to belong. It is imprinted on our DNA, it is stitched into our souls, it occupies our minds, it is the cry of our hearts.

My hope for you is that you continue to journey with what it means to belong and that you might not give up on this journey. It can be exhilarating, and it can be deeply painful, but what you are searching for is worth the journey.

James Martin, SJ reminds us: 'A deepening intimacy with God frees you to be honest with yourself and others.'[22] It is as we find that deep intimacy with God, as we belong to God, that we can honestly belong to others, ourselves and the world. That intimacy breaks into our reality today. That belonging in which we will find our deepest home, is so vast, powerful and deep that it cannot be contained by time and space. This belonging is rooted in the very heart of God himself, who is calling us, wooing us, reaching for us in every single moment. We may have to wait to experience the fullness of its depth, but finding our belonging in God is something available to us right in this moment.

As we wait for that revealing, we continue to journey and explore what it means to belong and catch magnificent glimpses of what that will be. It is a journey that we go on together, exploring who we are, why we are made, and where we are going. Ultimately, we are all walking each other home.

Notes

Foreword

1 Jen Baker's books by Authentic Media: *Face to Face* (Milton Keynes, 2019); *The Power of a Promise* (Milton Keynes, 2018).

1 Sitting Around the Fire

1 Mark and Lisa Scandrette, *Belonging and Becoming* (Oxford: Monarch, 2016), p. 82.
2 Either one or the other.
3 Genesis 2:19–20. Translation taken from Robert Alter, *The Five Books of Moses: A Translation with Commentary* (New York: W.W. Norton & Company Inc, 2004), p. 22.
4 Genesis 2:21–24. Translation taken from Robert Alter, *The Five Books of Moses*, pp. 22–3.
5 Psalm 33:20 NIV (my italics).
6 See notes in Robert Alter, *The Five Books of Moses*, p. 22.
7 Maori meeting house.
8 Jack Donovan, *Becoming a Barbarian* (Milwaukie: Dissonant Hum, 2016), p. 92.
9 Susan Pinker, *The Village Effect: Why Face to Face Contact Matters* (London: Atlantic Books, 2014), p. 7.

10 David Berreby, 'Why Do We See So Many Things As "Us Vs. Them"?' (*National Geographic* Online, https://www.national geographic.com/magazine/2018/04/things-that-divide-us, Accessed 23rd October 2019).

11 Toko-pa Turner, *Belonging: Remembering Ourselves Home* (Salt Spring Island: Her Own Room Press, 2017), p. 16.

12 James Martin, SJ, *Becoming Who You Are* (Mahwah: Hidden Spring, 2006), p. 83.

13 Psalm 42:7.

14 Thomas Merton, *No Man Is An Island* (Orlando: Harcourt Brace & Company, 1955), p. 126.

15 Thomas Merton, *No Man Is An Island*, p. 117.

2 What Happens When We Don't Belong?

1 Jo Swinney, *Home: The Quest to Belong* (London: Hodder & Stoughton, 2017), p. 17.

2 Cognitive Behavioural Therapy.

3 Turner, *Belonging*, p. 30.

4 Turner, *Belonging*, p. 21.

5 1 Corinthians 10:13a.

6 Patrick Regan, *Honesty Over Silence: It's OK Not to be OK* (Farnham: CWR, 2018), p. 24.

7 1 Corinthians 10:13b.

8 Turner, *Belonging*, p. 25.

9 All the Lonely People, Age UK 2018 quoted in www.campaign toendloneliness.org/the-facts-on-loneliness/.

10 www.relate.org.uk/sites/default/files/the_way_we_are_now_-_youre_not_alone.pdf.

11 Research presented at the 2017 convention for the American Psychological Association and view at www.mentalfloss.com/article/503378/research-suggests-loneliness-bad-you-smoking-nearly-pack-cigarettes-day.

12 Luke 15:11–24.

13 Luke 15:18.

14 Luke 15:19.

15 Charles L. Whitfield, *Healing the Child Within: Discovery and Recovery for Adult Children of Dysfunctional Families* (Deerfield Beach: Health Communications Inc, 1987), p. 45.

16 Luke 15:20.

17 Tom Wright, *Luke for Everyone* (London: SPCK, 2001), p. 187.

18 *Kezazah* literally means 'cutting off'.

3 Belonging to Yourself

1 Brené Brown, *Braving the Wilderness: The Quest for True Belonging and the Courage to Stand Alone* (London: Vermilion, 2017), p. 32.

2 Kat Seney-Williams, *Surviving and Thriving: On the Single-Parent Journey* (Oxford: Lion Hudson Limited, 2019), p. 12.

3 Kat Seney-Williams, *Surviving and Thriving*, p. 48.

4 Charles L. Whitfield, *A Gift to Myself* (Deerfield Beach, Health Communications Inc, 1990), p. 19.

5 Psalm 139:13–14 from Robert Alter, *The Book of Psalms: A Translation with Commentary* (New York: W.W. Norton and Company, 2007), p. 481.

6 Robert Alter, *The Book of Psalms*, p. 481.

7 1 John 3:1a.

8 See discussion in J. Philip Newell, *Christ of the Celts: The Healing of Creation* (Glasgow: Wild Goose Publications, 2008), p.29.

9 J. Philip Newell, *Christ of the Celts*, p. 29.

10 Ephesians 3:18–19.

11 Matthew 22:34–40.

12 Elayne Savage, *Don't Take it Personally: The Art of Dealing with Rejection* (New York: Open Road Distribution, 2016), p. 32.

13 Gary Chapman, *The Five Love Languages: How to Express Heartfelt Commitment to Your Mate* (Chicago: Northfield Publishing Co., 2004), p. 19.

14 Isaiah 43:1–3a.

15 Joyce Meyer, *Approval Addiction: Overcoming Your Need to Please Everyone* (London: Hodder & Stoughton, 2007), p. 66.

[16] Patrick Dodson, *Stuff My Dad Never Told Me About Relationships* (Auckland: Pause for Effect Limited, 2009), p. 24.

[17] 1 Corinthians 13:4–8a.

[18] Brené Brown, *Braving the Wilderness*, p. 40.

[19] Brené Brown, *Braving the Wilderness*, p. 32.

4 Thicker than Water?

[1] Nicky and Sila Lee, *The Parenting Book* (London: Alpha International, 2009), p. 19.

[2] Mark and Lisa Scandrette, *Belonging and Becoming: Creating a Thriving Family Culture* (Oxford: Lion Hudson Limited, 2016), p. 106.

[3] Genesis 2:24 NIV.

[4] Mark and Lisa Scandrette, *Belonging and Becoming*, p. 61.

[5] See point 14 at https://thoughtcatalog.com/nico-lang/2013/09/31-famous-quotations-youve-been-getting-wrong/.

[6] John 19:25–27 NIV.

[7] Ephesians 1:4b–5 NIV.

[8] 1 John 3:1 NIV.

[9] Jasmin Lee Cori, *The Emotionally Absent Mother: A Guide to Self-healing and Getting the Love You Missed* (New York: The Experiment, 2010), p. 108.

[10] David Coleman, *The Thriving Family: How to Achieve Lasting Home-Life Harmony for You and Your Children* (Dublin: Hachette Books Ireland, 2012), p. 19.

[11] Genesis 37:2–4 *The Message*.

[12] Robert Alter, *The Five Books of Moses: A Translation and Commentary* (New York: W.W. Norton & Company, 2004), pp. 206–7.

[13] Genesis 44:20 *The Message* (italics mine).

[14] David Coleman, *The Thriving Family*, p. 19.

5 The Community of the Church

1 Gilbert Bilezikian, *Community 101: Reclaiming the Local Church as Community of Oneness* (Grand Rapids: Zondervan, 1997), p. 59.

2 Leonard Sweet, *The Gospel According to Starbucks: Living with a Grande Passion* (Colorado Springs: Waterbrook Press, 2007), p. 129.

3 John 13:34–35 NIV.

4 Romans 12:3–10 NIV.

5 Philippians 2:3b–4 NIV.

6 Rick Warren, *The Purpose Driven Life: What On Earth Am I Here For?* (Grand Rapids: Zondervan, 2002), p. 265.

7 Jean Vanier, *Community and Growth* (London: Darton, Longman & Todd Ltd, 2006), p. 19.

8 1 Corinthians 12:12–31 NIV.

9 Selwyn Hughes, *Discovering Your Place in the Body of Christ* (London: Marshall Paperbacks, 1982), p. 11.

10 See Dennis Linn, Sheila Fabricant Linn & Matthew Linn, *What is My Song* (New York: Paulist Press, 2005).

11 See Dennis Linn, Sheila Fabricant Linn & Matthew Linn, *Healing the Purpose of Your Life* (New York: Paulist Press, 1999).

12 Dennis Linn, Sheila Fabricant Linn & Matthew Linn, *Healing the Purpose of Your Life*, p. 48.

13 Jean Vanier, *Community and Growth* (London: Darton, Longman & Todd Ltd, 2006), pp. 16–17.

14 Romans 15:7 NIV.

15 Jürgen Moltmann, *The Open Church: Invitation to a Messianic Life-style* (London: SCM Press Ltd, 1983) p. 27.

16 John 13:35.

17 Mark 10:17–22.

18 John 14:1.

19 Galatians 5:22–23a NIV.

20 Joseph Myers, *The Search to Belong: Rethinking Intimacy, Community and Small Groups* (Grand Rapids: Zondervan, 2003), p. 27.

6 Belonging to God

[1] Richard Rohr, *The Divine Dance* (London: SPCK, 2016), p. 109.
[2] Nigel G. Wright, *God on the Inside: The Holy Spirit in Holy Scripture* (Oxford: The Bible Reading Fellowship, 2006), p. 17–18.
[3] See Wayne Grudem, *Systematic Theology* (Grand Rapids: Zondervan, 1994), p. 248.
[4] Deuteronomy 6:4 NIV.
[5] Tim Chester, *Delighting in the Trinity: Just Why Are Father, Son and Spirit Such Good News?* (Oxford: Monarch Books, 2005), p. 26.
[6] Wright, *God on the Inside*, p. 21.
[7] 1 John 4:8.
[8] 1 John 3:1 NIV.
[9] Matthew 7:9–11 NIV.
[10] Mark 14:36 NIV.
[11] Isaiah 43:1.
[12] Ephesians 2:13 NLV.
[13] Romans 8:29 NIV.
[14] R.T. Kendall, *The Sensitivity of the Spirit* (London: Hodder & Stoughton, 2000), p. 147.
[15] Luke 4:1 NIV.
[16] Kendall, *The Sensitivity of the Spirit*, p. 26.
[17] Galatians 4:6–7.
[18] John 17:20–26 NIV.
[19] John 17:21 NIV.
[20] Psalm 133:1–3 NIV.
[21] Gary M. Burge, *John: The NIV Application Commentary* (Grand Rapids: Zondervan, 2000), p. 468.
[22] John 17:21 NIV.
[23] Genesis 18:1–8.
[24] Richard Rohr, *The Divine Dance* (London: SPCK, 2016), p. 31.
[25] See Rohr, *The Divine Dance*, p. 55.
[26] See Rohr, *The Divine Dance*, pp. 91–2.
[27] Rohr, *The Divine Dance*, p. 92.

[28] See Diarmuid O'Murchu, *Quantum Theology: Spiritual Implications of the New Physics* (New York: The Crossroad Publishing Company, 1998), p. 66.

[29] O'Murchu, *Quantum Theology*, pp. 194–5.

[30] Acts 17:28 NIV.

[31] O'Murchu, *Quantum Theology*, p. 76.

[32] Ephesians 3:18–19.

7 What a Wonderful World

[1] David Adam, *The Rhythm of Life: Celtic Daily Prayer* (London: SPCK, 1996), p. 30.

[2] Genesis 1:4,10,12,18,21,24.

[3] Genesis 1:31a.

[4] Norman Wirzba, *From Nature to Creation: A Christian Vision for Understanding and Loving our World* (Grand Rapids: Baker Books, 2015), p. 10.

[5] Wirzba, *From Nature to Creation*, p. 30.

[6] J. Philip Newell, *Christ of the Celts: The Healing of Creation* (Glasgow: Wild Goose Publications, 2008), p. 59.

[7] Genesis 1:2b NIV.

[8] Article written by Tammana Begum, https://www.nhm.ac.uk/discover/news/2019/december/humans-are-causing-life-on-earth-to-vanish.html, published December 2019.

[9] Damien Carrington, https://www.theguardian.com/environment/2018/may/21/human-race-just-001-of-all-life-but-has-destroyed-over-80-of-wild-mammals-study, published May 2018.

[10] Robert S. White, *Creation in Crisis: Christian Perspectives on Sustainability* (SPCK: London, 2009), p. 1.

[11] We have been really blessed to partner with A Rocha, a Christian charity working for the protection and restoration of the natural world, and who are committed to mobilising Christians and churches in the UK to care for the environment. We have recently been awarded their Eco-Church silver award.

[12] Colossians 1:20 *The Message*.

13 Romans 8:19–21 *The Message*.
14 Romans 8:22.
15 Newell, *Christ of the Celts*, p. 63.
16 See discussion in Andy Percey, *Infused with Life: Exploring God's Gift of Rest in a World of Busyness* (Milton Keynes: Authentic, 2019), pp. 23–5.
17 Genesis 1:26–29.
18 1 Chronicles 29:10b–11.
19 Psalm 24:1–2.
20 Psalm 145:9 (italics mine).
21 Leviticus 25:23–24.

8 Ruth: A Story of the Ordinary

1 Ruth 1:1–5.
2 Ruth 1:6–18.
3 Exodus 3:7–8a.
4 John 21:3.
5 Deuteronomy 6:23 NIV.
6 For further comment see Robert Alter, *The Hebrew Bible – The Writings: A Translation with Commentary* (New York: W.W. Norton & Company, 2019), p. 627.
7 See Genesis 32:26.
8 Ruth 4:12 NKJV.
9 Ruth 1:22; 2:2; 2:21; 4:5; 4:10.
10 Ruth 2:1–7.
11 Deuteronomy 24:19–22 NIV.
12 Deuteronomy 14:28–29 NIV.
13 Leviticus 19:9–10 NIV.
14 Deuteronomy 10:18 NIV.
15 David Atkinson, *BST Commentary Series: The Message of Ruth* (Leicester: Inter-Varsity Press, 1983), p. 60.
16 Chris Seay, *A Place at the Table: 40 Days of Solidarity with the Poor* (Grand Rapids: Baker Books, 2012), p. 18.
17 Ruth 4:9–12.

[18] Ruth 4:17b.

[19] Colossians 1:19 *The Message*.

9 The Great Revealing

[1] Frank Cooke, *Living in the Covenant: The Basis of Our Relationship with God* (Eastbourne: Kingsway Publications, 1989), p. 122.

[2] Rob Bell, *What is the Bible?: How an Ancient Library of Poems, Letters and Stories Can Transform the Way You Think and Feel About Everything* (London: William Collins, 2017), p. 203.

[3] Revelation 7:9–12.

[4] Genesis 15:5 NIV.

[5] Nick Page, *A Nearly Infallible History of Christianity: Being a History of 2000 Years of Saints, Sinners, Idiots and Divinely-inspired Troublemakers* (London: Hodder & Stoughton, 2013), p. 384.

[6] Galatians 3:28.

[7] Jürgen Moltmann, *Theology of Hope* (London: SCM Press Ltd, 1967), p. 224.

[8] Revelation 22:1–5.

[9] Isaiah 65:17.

[10] 2 Peter 3:8–13.

[11] See Genesis 1.

[12] 2 Peter 3:10 KJV (italics mine).

[13] See Ruth Valero, *Eschatology and the Environment*, in Stephen Holmes and Russell Rook, *What Are We Waiting For?: Christian Hope and Contemporary Culture* (Milton Keynes: Paternoster, 2008), pp. 206–7.

[14] See Ruth Valero, *Eschatology and the Environment*, in Stephen Holmes and Russell Rook, *What Are We Waiting For?*, p. 207.

[15] Rob Bell, *What is the Bible?*, p. 202.

[16] Revelation 21:1–5.

[17] 1 Corinthians 13:12.

[18] David Bentley Hart, *The Doors of the Sea: Where Was God in the Tsunami?* (Grand Rapids: William B. Eerdmans Publishing Company, 2005), p. 104.

19 Joseph R. Myers, *The Search to Belong: Rethinking Intimacy, Community and Small Groups* (Grand Rapids: Zondervan, 2003), p. 30.

20 2 Corinthians 5:4–5 *The Message*.

21 C.H. Spurgeon, *Spurgeon's Sermons* Volume 54 (a sermon published January 1908).

22 James Martin, SJ, *Becoming Who You Are* (Boston: Hidden Spring, 2006), p. 49.

Bibliography

Adam, D., *The Rhythm of Life: Celtic Daily Prayer* (London: SPCK, 1996).

Alter, R., *The Book of Psalms: A Translation with Commentary* (New York: W.W. Norton and Company, 2007).

Alter, R., *The Five Books of Moses: A Translation with Commentary* (New York: W.W. Norton & Company, 2004).

Alter, R., *The Hebrew Bible – The Writings: A Translation with Commentary* (New York: W.W. Norton & Company, 2019).

Atkinson, D., *BST Commentary Series: The Message of Ruth* (Leicester: Inter-Varsity Press, 1983).

Begum, T., https://www.nhm.ac.uk/discover/news/2019/december/humans-are-causing-life-on-earth-to-vanish.html, published December 2019.

Bell, R., *What is the Bible?: How an Ancient Library of Poems, Letters and Stories Can Transform the Way You Think and Feel About Everything* (London: William Collins, 2017).

Bentley Hart, D., *The Doors of the Sea: Where Was God in the Tsunami?* (Grand Rapids: William B. Eerdmans Publishing Company, 2005).

Berreby, D., 'Why Do We See So Many Things As "Us Vs. Them"?' (*National Geographic* Online, https://www.national geographic.com/magazine/2018/04/things-that-divide-us, accessed 23rd October 2019).

Bilezikian, G., *Community 101: Reclaiming the Local Church as Community of Oneness* (Grand Rapids: Zondervan, 1997).

Brown, B., *Braving the Wilderness: The Quest for True Belonging and the Courage to Stand Alone* (London: Vermilion, 2017).

Burge, G.M., *John: The NIV Application Commentary* (Grand Rapids: Zondervan, 2000).

Carrington, D., https://www.theguardian.com/environment/2018/may/21/human-race-just-001-of-all-life-but-has-destroyed-over-80-of-wild-mammals-study, published May 2018.

Chapman, G., *The Five Love Languages: How to Express Heartfelt Commitment to Your Mate* (Chicago: Northfield Publishing Co, 2004).

Chester, T., *Delighting in the Trinity: Just Why Are Father, Son and Spirit Such Good News?* (Oxford: Monarch Books, 2005).

Coleman, D., *The Thriving Family: How to Achieve Lasting Home-Life Harmony for You and Your Children* (Dublin: Hachette Books Ireland, 2012).

Cooke, F., *Living in the Covenant: The Basis of Our Relationship with God* (Eastbourne: Kingsway Publications, 1989).

Dodson, P., *Stuff My Dad Never Told Me About Relationships* (Auckland: Pause for Effect Limited, 2009).

Donovan, J., *Becoming a Barbarian* (Milwaukie: Dissonant Hum, 2016).

Grudem, W., *Systematic Theology* (Grand Rapids: Zondervan, 1994).

Hughes, S., *Discovering Your Place in the Body of Christ* (London: Marshall Paperbacks, 1982).

Kendall, R.T., *The Sensitivity of the Spirit* (London: Hodder & Stoughton, 2000).

Cori, J.L., *The Emotionally Absent Mother: A Guide to Self-healing and Getting the Love You Missed* (New York: The Experiment, 2010).

Lee, N. and S., *The Parenting Book* (London: Alpha International, 2009).

Linn, D. and M., and S. Fabricant Linn, *Healing the Purpose of Your Life* (New York: Paulist Press, 1999).

Linn, D. and M., and S. Fabricant Linn, *What is My Song* (New York: Paulist Press, 2005).

Martin SJ, J., *Becoming Who You Are* (Mahwah: Hidden Spring, 2006).

Merton, T., *No Man is an Island* (Orlando: Harcourt Brace & Company, 1955).

Meyer, J., *Approval Addiction: Overcoming Your Need to Please Everyone* (London: Hodder & Stoughton, 2007).

Moltmann, J., *The Open Church: Invitation to a Messianic Life-style* (London: SCM Press Ltd, 1983).

Moltmann, J., *Theology of Hope* (London: SCM Press Ltd, 1967).

Myers, J., *The Search to Belong: Rethinking Intimacy, Community and Small Groups* (Grand Rapids: Zondervan, 2003).

Newell, J.P., *Christ of the Celts: The Healing of Creation* (Glasgow: Wild Goose Publications, 2008).

O'Murchu, D., *Quantum Theology: Spiritual Implications of the New Physics* (New York: The Crossroad Publishing Company, 1998).

Page, N., *A Nearly Infallible History of Christianity: Being a History of 2000 Years of Saints, Sinners, Idiots and Divinely-inspired Troublemakers* (London: Hodder & Stoughton, 2013).

Percey, A., *Infused with Life: Exploring God's Gift of Rest in a World of Busyness* (Milton Keynes: Authentic, 2019).

Pinker, S., *The Village Effect: Why Face-to-Face Contact Matters* (London: Atlantic Books, 2014).

Regan, P., *Honesty Over Silence: It's OK Not to be OK* (Farnham: CWR, 2018).

Rohr, R., *The Divine Dance* (London: SPCK, 2016).

Savage, E., *Don't Take it Personally: The Art of Dealing with Rejection* (New York: Open Road Distribution, 2016).

Scandrette, M. and L., *Belonging and Becoming* (Oxford: Monarch, 2016).

Seay, C., *A Place at the Table: 40 Days of Solidarity with the Poor* (Grand Rapids: Baker Books, 2012).

Seney-Williams, K., *Surviving and Thriving: On the Single-Parent Journey* (Oxford: Lion Hudson Limited, 2019).

Sweet, L., *The Gospel According to Starbucks: Living with a Grande Passion* (Colorado Springs: Waterbrook Press, 2007).

Swinney, J., *Home: The Quest to Belong* (London: Hodder & Stoughton, 2017).

Turner, Toko-pa, *Belonging: Remembering Ourselves Home* (Salt Spring Island: Her Own Room Press, 2017).

Valero, R., *Eschatology and the Environment*, in Stephen Holmes and Russell Rook, *What Are We Waiting For?: Christian Hope and Contemporary Culture* (Milton Keynes: Paternoster, 2008).

Vanier, J., *Community and Growth* (London: Darton, Longman & Todd Ltd, 2006).

Warren, R., *The Purpose Driven Life: What On Earth Am I Here For?* (Grand Rapids: Zondervan, 2002).

White, R.S., *Creation in Crisis: Christian Perspectives on Sustainability* (SPCK: London, 2009).

Whitfield, C.L., *A Gift to Myself* (Deerfield Beach: Health Communications Inc, 1990).

Whitfield, C.L., *Healing the Child Within: Discovery and Recovery for Adult Children of Dysfunctional Families* (Deerfield Beach: Health Communications Inc, 1987).

Wirzba, N., *From Nature to Creation: A Christian Vision for Understanding and Loving our World* (Grand Rapids: Baker Books, 2015).

Wright, N.G., *God on the Inside: The Holy Spirit in Holy Scripture* (Oxford: The Bible Reading Fellowship, 2006).

Wright, T., *Luke for Everyone* (London: SPCK, 2001).